THE IDEAL HOME SHOW SEASONAL COOK BOOK

OVER 100 RECIPES, TIPS, TECHNIQUES AND BRILLIANT IDEAS

ideal
HOME SHOW

THE IDEAL
HOME SHOW
SEASONAL
COOK
BOOK

OVER 100 RECIPES, TIPS,
TECHNIQUES AND BRILLIANT IDEAS

First published in Great Britain in 2013 by Media 10 Ltd

Media 10 Ltd
Crown House
151 High Road
Loughton
IG10 4LF

www.media-ten.com

A CIP catalogue record for this book is available
from the British Library

ISBN: 978-0-9575374-0-8

Media 10 Ltd
Chief executive   Lee Newton
Co-ordinator   Kerry Garwood
Production director   Tim Garwood

Design and art direction   Nigel Wright
Project editor   Hilary Ivory
Photography   Ruth Jenkinson
                           David Munns
Home economy   Emma Marsden
                           Ellie Jarvis
Contributing writer   Felicity Cloake

Printed and bound in the UK by Butler Tanner & Dennis

Contents

Created in 1908, still reflecting British life over a hundred years later

The Ideal Home Show has been a barometer of change ever since it first opened its doors to the public.

When the Ideal Home Show made its debut at the beginning of the last century, the Suffragettes were protesting in the name of women's rights, Model T Fords were on a production line in Manchester, and Britain's first skyscraper, the 90m Royal Liver Building, was going up in Liverpool. Fast-forward to 2013 and we've had the Occupy movement in the name of economic justice, electric cars appearing on our roads and Britain's tallest building, the 308m Shard, dominating London's skyline.

As well as being a launch pad for cutting-edge gadgetry and the latest in contemporary living (the vacuum cleaner, electric kettle, toaster and Teasmade were all unveiled to an astonished public at the Ideal Home Exhibition, as it was then known), it has welcomed HRH Queen Elizabeth II on eleven occasions, along with other Royals and a host of notables and celebrities.

Food was then, as it is now, a major attraction – the Ideal Home Show has always showcased the best of British produce. This begs the question: what exactly is British cuisine? We believe that it's a glorious mix of all the cultural influences that make up this nation's history. From the spicy influences of India through to the sunny flavours of the Caribbean, we are a melting pot of world cuisine, and we're proud of it!

HAPPY 100th birthday
IDEAL HOME SHOW

Celebrating 100 years of inspiration
1908 to 2008

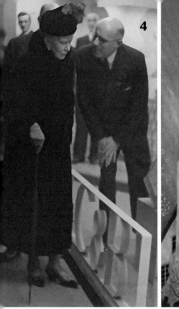

IDEAL HOME EXHIBITION

1950

CATALOGUE
and
REVIEW

1) An early Hovis stand – the millers claimed their bread had 'flesh-forming and bone-making properties'... 2) A 1920s 'dishwasher': plates and dishes were loaded into the rack and hosed with hot water at pressure! 3) Cooking demonstrations are a big attraction. 4) Queen Mary (Queen Elizabeth's grandmother) at the 1947 Exhibition. 5) A cooker by Trinity Cookers for bedsit living, 1955. 6) The 2012 Ideal Home Show being opened by Prince Charles in the company of (left to right) Lee Newton (Chief Executive of Ideal Home Show owner, Media 10), George Clarke, Myleene Klass, Laurence Llewelyn-Bowen, Suzi Perry and Gregg Wallace. 7) The Queen and Prince Philip on one of many visits over the years.

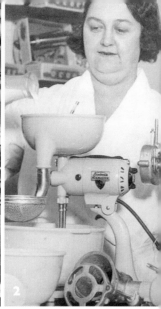

1) This 'bathtub' at the 1996 Exhibition held two full-sized canal boats, one of them an ultra-modern model that was also a *Daily Mail* competition prize. 2) The new Sunbeam Mixmaster is put through its paces at the 1934 Exhibition. 3) Queen Elizabeth II at the Ideal Home Exhibition, 1949. 4) Sid James and Diana Coupland, stars of the TV series *Bless This House*, at a 1973 Exhibition show house. 5) Raymond Blanc wows the crowds. 6) The fashion for fitted kitchens with all mod cons took off in the Seventies. 7) Gregg Wallace has a whale of a time doing what he does best at the 2012 Show. 8) Prince Charles. 9) Gino D'Acampo cooks up a storm. 10) Actress Eileen Pollock tries out an electric washing machine in 1935. 11) With the trompe l'oeil façade of Earls Court Exhibition Centre providing a stunning backdrop, the Band of the Scots Guards put on a rousing musical display. 12) Martin Blunos in full show-time demo swing.

SPRING

BEST IN SEASON

SPRING

March

Cabbage (green), chicory, leeks, mushrooms, purple sprouting broccoli, rhubarb (forced), sea kale, spring greens, winter greens

Hare, lamb

Cockles, crab, pollock, rock oysters, sea trout, wild salmon

April

Cabbage (green), cauliflower, Jersey Royal potatoes, lettuce, mushrooms (including St George's and wild morels), purple sprouting broccoli, radishes, rhubarb (forced and outdoor), sea kale, spring greens, watercress, winter greens

Lamb, wood pigeon

Cockles, crab, pollock, sea trout, wild salmon

May

Asparagus, cabbage (green), carrots, cauliflower, elderflower, Jersey Royal potatoes, lettuce, mushrooms (including wild morels), radish, rhubarb (outdoor), rocket, sea kale, sorrel, watercress, wild garlic

Lamb, wood pigeon

Cuttlefish, freshwater crayfish, pollock, sea trout, spider and brown crab, wild salmon

Spring

Starters

Watercress, pea and mint soup	16
Pan-fried shellfish with lime	18
Speedy Thai fish cakes	22
Manhattan clam chowder	24
Asparagus with preserved lemon and paprika aioli (V)	26
Baked garlic pizza bread (V)	28

Mains

Quick-to-make chicken filo parcels	32
Sole with spinach in tomato sauce	34
Spinach and goat's cheese tart (V)	36
Chicken satay with spicy peanut sauce	38
Smoked trout, potato and caper salad	40
Potato Gorgonzola pizza (V)	42
Chicken and spicy arrabbiata sauce with pasta	44
Posh lamb stew	46
Roast duck with orange and caramelised shallots	50
Seafood stew with king prawns, clams and sea bass	52
Poussins with a honey and lemon glaze	54
Italian-style saucy spare ribs	56
Simple saltimbocca	58
Spicy kebabs with simple sides	60
Lamb boulangère	62
Spring side dishes that go with everything (V)	64

Puddings & bakes

Hot cross buns	66
Rhubarb lollies	68
Easiest-ever chocolate tart	70
Fresh elderflower cordial with ginger and lime	72

IDEAL MENU SUGGESTION

Watercress, pea and mint soup
Try a white Rioja from Spain or a New Zealand Sauvignon Blanc

Lamb boulangère
A South African Cabernet Sauvignon/Merlot or Bordeaux Cru Bourgeois
will balance the lamb

Easiest-ever chocolate tart

ideal
TRUSTED FOR
HOME SHOW
OVER 100 YEARS

Watercress, pea and mint soup

Watercress is at its seasonal best in spring, a welcome signal that winter is at an end. It's delicious tossed in salads, used as a creamy sauce for salmon, or made into a soup that marries wonderfully with sweet peas and fragrant mint.

prep 10 mins cook 30 mins SERVES 4-6

ingredients

25g butter
1 tbsp olive oil
1 small onion, finely chopped
1 medium potato, around 150g,
    chopped
200g frozen peas, thawed
2-3 tbsp fresh mint or 1 tbsp
    mint jelly or mint sauce
Pinch of sugar
1 litre hot chicken stock
100g bag watercress, chopped
Salt and freshly ground black
    pepper
4 tbsp single or double cream

1 Melt the butter in a pan with the oil over a medium heat. Add the onion and cook gently for about 15 minutes until softened. Add the potato, peas, mint, sugar and stock and bring to the boil. Simmer gently, half covered, until the potato is really tender. Stir in the watercress and cook for 1-2 minutes.

2 Purée the soup in a food processor. Return it to the pan and gently reheat, seasoning to taste. Stir in a little of the cream, and serve with crusty bread.

"For an ultra-smooth, restaurant-style texture, blend the soup as above and then sieve it back into the saucepan. Discard the bits left in the sieve and reheat gently."

Pan-fried shellfish with lime

The secret to cooking shellfish really well is to get the pan very hot before you start to cook them. The texture you're looking for in cooked scallops is seared on the outside and meltingly soft in the middle, while prawns should turn from grey to pink and opaque.

prep 8 mins cook 5 mins SERVES 4

ingredients

8-12 large fresh scallops, with or without coral
1 large juicy lime
3 tbsp olive oil
15g butter
175g large shelled prawns
Salt and freshly ground black pepper
2 tbsp chopped chives or spring onion tops

1 If the scallops still have the coral attached, carefully cut them apart and pat dry. Cut very large scallops into two thick slices.

2 Slice the lime very thinly. Heat a non-stick pan with the oil and butter. Once the butter has stopped foaming, add the lime slices first, pressing gently to release a little juice.

3 Add the scallops and cook for 1 minute each side. Add the prawns and season well. Cook for a further minute or two until the scallops are just milky white and almost firm.

4 Spoon into bowls, top with the chives or spring onion tops and serve at once with crusty bread and a crisp green salad.

"Time is of the essence when cooking shellfish, as it cooks in minutes. Prepare all the fish before cooking and make sure your pan is hot - you want to hear a sizzle when shellfish hit the pan."

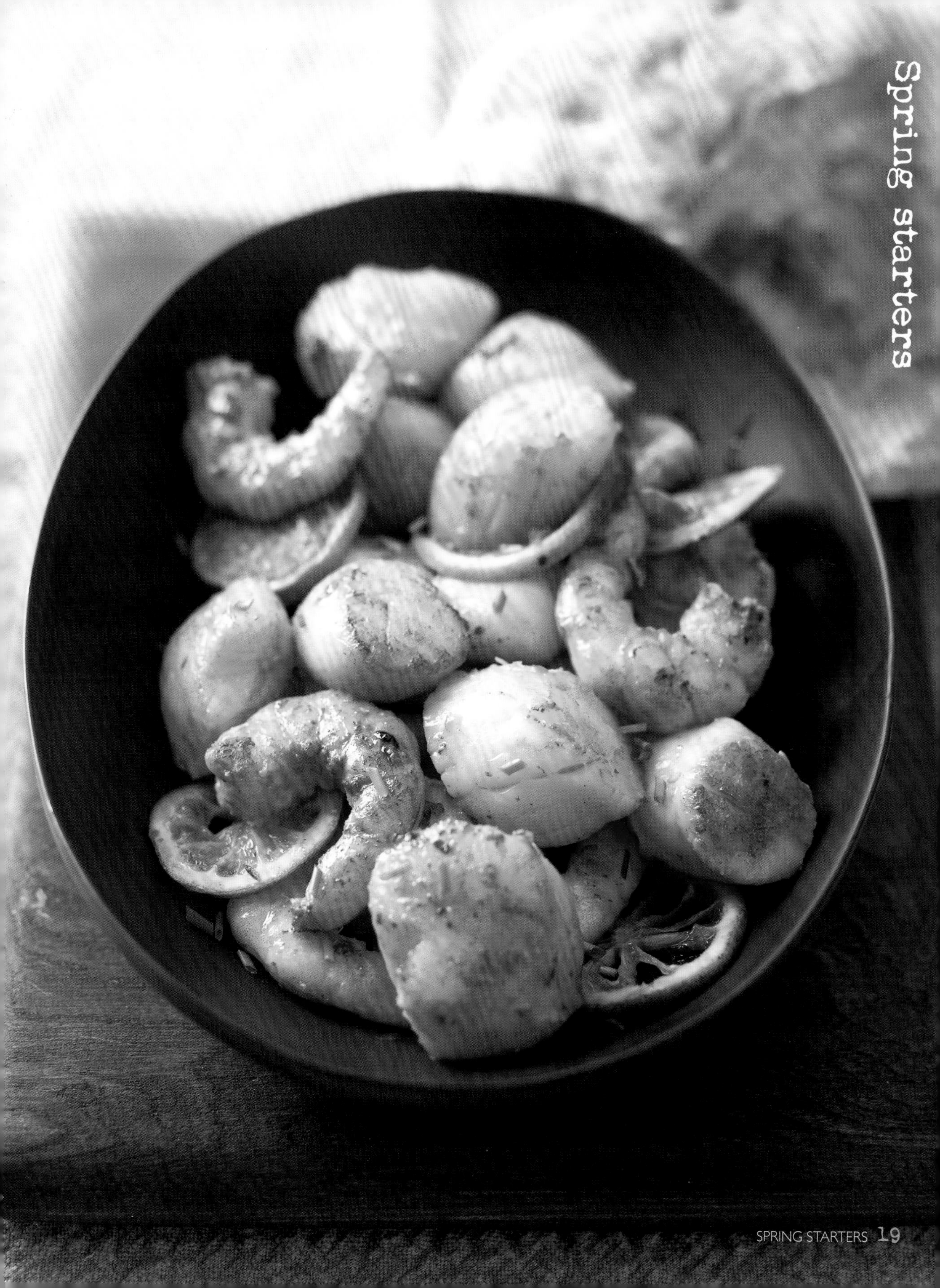

Spring starters

TOP TIP
Griddled, roasted or steamed, asparagus is a quintessentially British vegetable that has a very short season. Enjoy it with a drizzle of olive oil and balsamic vinegar, or a knob of butter and a squeeze of lemon juice.

MORE SPRING STARTERS ▶

Speedy Thai fish cakes

This is the recipe to have up your sleeve for lunch on the fly with a friend, or a starter with oomph. You need only a handful of ingredients with a flavour-boosting dollop of Thai curry paste, and it's ready to serve with chilli dipping sauce.

prep 10 mins cook 5 mins SERVES 4

ingredients

12 fine green beans
250g fresh or canned crabmeat,
    drained
2 tbsp good mayonnaise
2 tbsp freshly chopped
    coriander
2 tsp Thai red curry paste
4 tbsp fresh white breadcrumbs
2 tbsp groundnut oil
Thai chilli dipping sauce

1 Bring a small pan of water to the boil and drop in the beans. Cook for 1 minute, then drain well and cool quickly under cold running water. Chop finely.

2 Put the beans in a bowl, add the crabmeat (if using canned, drain well first), the mayonnaise, coriander and curry paste.

3 Stir in half the breadcrumbs. Take a spoonful of the mixture and shape into rounds a little bigger than an apricot. Roll each in the remaining breadcrumbs, patting them all round into a neat shape. Freeze for 10 minutes if you have time.

4 Heat the groundnut oil in a pan and fry the cakes gently for 1-2 minutes until golden brown on both sides. Serve immediately with a bowlful of Thai dipping sauce.

"For a canapé, use a teaspoon to scoop up the mixture and make them bite-sized. Serve in individual Little Gem leaves topped with a spoonful of Thai dipping sauce and a coriander leaf to garnish."

Manhattan clam chowder

This rich North American stew is a meal in itself. It can be creamy and packed with corn or fishy like this one, which has a tomato base and is chock-a-block with vegetables. If you can't get fresh clams, use two cans of well-drained baby clams, or a bag of mussels.

prep 15 mins cook 1 hour SERVES 6

ingredients

24 clams, washed and drained
1.7 litres light fish stock
1 tbsp olive oil
15g unsalted butter
4 rashers streaky bacon, diced
3 carrots, diced
3 celery sticks, diced
1 onion, finely chopped
1 green pepper, diced
2 garlic cloves, crushed
1 tbsp thyme leaves, roughly
   chopped
1 bay leaf
Pinch of cayenne pepper
Salt and freshly ground black
   pepper
2 x 400g tins chopped tomatoes
2 large potatoes, cut into bite-
   size cubes
1 tbsp flat-leaf parsley, roughly
   chopped

1 Place the fresh clams in a large pan, pour in the fish stock and cover with a lid. Bring to a simmer and heat until the shells open, around 5-7 minutes. Drain well, reserving the liquid. Set the clams aside to cool.

2 Heat the olive oil with the butter in the same pan and when hot fry the bacon until golden. Add the carrots, celery, onion, green pepper, garlic, thyme, bay leaf and cayenne pepper. Season well. Cook the vegetables for around 5 minutes until they're just soft, but not coloured.

3 Remove the clams from their shells and discard the shells. Pour the reserved fish stock over the vegetables, add the tomatoes and potatoes, then allow the mixture to simmer over a very low heat for approximately 1 hour, finally adding the clams and any juice for the last 5 minutes.

4 To serve, ladle into warm bowls, sprinkle with parsley and serve immediately with warm crusty bread.

"Turn this into a seriously good fish stew with chunks of salmon, monkfish and prawns. Add them at the end of Step 3, pushing the fish down underneath the liquid so that it cooks gently in the heat."

Asparagus with preserved lemon and paprika aioli

There's nothing to beat the taste of fresh English asparagus tossed in butter and seasoning and served with a squeeze of lemon. To transform it into a sublime starter, serve with a dollop of creamy aioli, made with preserved lemons and flavoured with paprika.

prep 15-20 mins cook 5 mins SERVES 6

ingredients

2 egg yolks
100ml olive oil, plus extra to drizzle
200ml vegetable oil
1 preserved lemon, halved and deseeded
½ tsp paprika
½ garlic clove, crushed
Juice and zest of ½ lemon
Salt and freshly ground black pepper
3 bundles of asparagus
Crusty bread, to serve

1 Put the egg yolks in a bowl and beat with a balloon whisk or electric beater to break down the yolks.

2 Drizzle a small amount of the olive oil and vegetable oil onto the egg yolks and whisk in, adding a bit more, little by little, until the mixture forms an emulsion. As soon as it has thickened and looks glossy, you can add the oil in slightly bigger quantities. Take care not to add too much in one go or the mixture will separate.

3 Finely chop the preserved lemon and add to the mayonnaise with the paprika, garlic, lemon zest and juice. Fold everything together and season with salt to taste.

4 Prepare the asparagus by trimming about 1cm of the stalk from each end. Use a vegetable peeler and, starting from the end, peel off about 2.5cm.

5 Bring a large pan of salted water to the boil and cook the asparagus for 3-4 minutes until just tender. Drain well, toss in a little olive oil and season with salt and pepper.

6 Arrange the asparagus on six starter plates, spoon the aioli into a bowl to have alongside, and serve with crusty bread.

Baked garlic pizza bread

These wafer-thin pizza slices slathered in garlic butter have 'cucina Italiana' stamped all over them. The secret is rolling the dough out until it's so thin it's practically transparent, and then baking it until it's crisp.

prep 20 mins cook 4-5 mins each batch SERVES 6

ingredients

375g strong bread flour
2 tsp salt, plus a little extra
1 tsp easy blend yeast
1 tsp caster sugar
1 tbsp light olive oil
75g butter, softened
2 garlic cloves, crushed
Chopped parsley

1 Sift the flour into a large bowl and stir in the salt. Mix the yeast and sugar with 100ml warm water, give it a stir and set aside for 10 minutes to dissolve the yeast.

2 Make a well in the middle of the flour mixture and pour in the yeast liquid with the olive oil and an extra 150ml warm water. Mix with a knife to make a craggy dough, then tip out onto a clean work surface and knead for about 10 minutes until soft, smooth and sticky. Shape into a round and transfer to a clean bowl. Cover and leave to prove for 30 minutes.

3 Preheat the oven to its hottest setting (if you have the option on your oven, choose the top and bottom setting for this) and put a baking sheet or pizza stone in to get really hot.

4 Beat the butter and garlic in a bowl with a pinch of salt.

5 Cut the dough into six even pieces. On a lightly floured, clean work surface, roll one piece out until it's really thin. Fold over into a neat square and then roll out again until it's super-thin.

6 Balance the rolled-out dough on a rolling pin and transfer to the preheated baking sheet. Brush with a little garlic butter and bake for 4-5 minutes until cooked through and bubbled on top. Sprinkle with parsley. Repeat until you've cooked all the dough, and serve. Eat while hot, as it will lose its crispness very soon. (But it can be reheated quickly in the oven, if need be.)

Celebrity chefs who cooked at
The Ideal Home Show

1) During his long career, chef **Martin Blunos** has held two Michelin stars.
2) **Theo Randall** is head chef at Theo Randall At The InterContinental, London.
3) **Juliet Sear** is the brains behind Fancy Nancy Cakes. 4) Chef and proprietor of Le Manoir aux Quat' Saisons since 1984, **Raymond Blanc** personifies gastronomic excellence. 5) **Henry** and **Tom Herbert** of Hobbs House Bakery featured in Channel 4's The Fabulous Baker Brothers in 2012.

5

4

SPRING MAINS ▶

Quick-to-make chicken filo parcels

This dish is all about texture – a crisp layer of baked filo pastry enveloping a succulent chicken breast stuffed with a soft, savoury filling. Served with steamed tender-stem broccoli and buttered new potatoes, it's an unbelievably tasty and satisfying main course.

prep 20 mins cook 30 mins SERVES 4

ingredients

15g butter or 1 tbsp oil
50g mushrooms, wiped and very
   finely diced
Zest of 1 lemon
25g wholemeal breadcrumbs
Salt and freshly ground black
   pepper
4 x 150g skinless, boneless
   chicken breasts
8 sheets filo pastry
Olive oil, for brushing
1 tsp sesame seed

1 Make the filling. Melt the butter or heat the oil in a pan and add the mushrooms. Cook until softened. Remove from the heat and stir in the lemon zest and breadcrumbs. Season well, and set aside to cool.

2 Preheat the oven to 180°C/160°C fan oven/gas mark 4. Lightly oil a baking sheet. Place the chicken breasts on a board and, with a sharp knife, carefully cut a pocket along the length of each. Divide the stuffing between the pockets.

3 On a separate board lay out a sheet of filo, brush it with oil and place another sheet over it. Put the chicken on top, season well, then wrap the filo around it and brush again with oil. Sprinkle with sesame seeds. Repeat for all the chicken breasts.

4 Place them on the prepared baking sheet and bake for 25 minutes until the pastry is golden and the chicken is cooked through.

Sole with spinach in tomato sauce

Thin, delicate fillets of sole cooked in minutes under a hot grill, teamed with a Mediterranean-inspired seasoning of orange, basil and capers in a thick tomato sauce. Serve with an avocado salad and buttered new potatoes.

prep 20 mins cook 8 mins SERVES 4

ingredients

Knob of butter, plus a little extra melted
1 garlic clove, crushed
400g can chopped tomatoes
100ml dry white wine
200ml hot vegetable stock
Pinch of sugar
Salt and freshly ground black pepper
1 tbsp capers
1 tbsp freshly chopped basil leaves
8 fillets of sole, skinned
About 50g fresh leaf spinach – small leaves, if possible
1 tsp orange zest and juice of 1 small orange

1 Melt the butter in a pan and cook the garlic just until you start to smell the aroma. Add the tomatoes, wine, stock and sugar, and season well. Bring to the boil and simmer for 15 minutes until thickened. Stir in the capers and basil. Preheat the grill.

2 Lay each fish fillet out flat and season, then place a couple of spinach leaves on top, and carefully roll up the fillet from the thinnest end. You could secure them in place with cocktail sticks, but there should be no need if the dish is not too big.

3 Divide the sauce between four small ovenproof dishes and place two rolled-up fillets in each. Sprinkle with some orange zest and juice, and drizzle a little melted butter over. Season again. Place under the hot grill and cook for 7-8 minutes or until the fish is tender when pierced with a knife, taking care not to let it burn or overcook.

Spinach and goat's cheese tart

Pots of soft, rindless goat's cheese are the ones to use here. The taste is subtle and creamy, and it goes brilliantly with the slightly bitter flavour of spinach.

prep 15 mins cook 40-50 mins SERVES 6-8

ingredients

175g plain flour
Salt and freshly ground black
    pepper
110g firm but not hard butter
1 tbsp olive oil
Bunch of spring onions, finely
    chopped
Leaves from a few sprigs of
    fresh thyme
200g small spinach leaves,
    roughly chopped, or trimmed
    watercress
300ml tub crème fraîche
3 large eggs
150g pot soft, rindless goat's
    cheese

1 Sieve the flour and a good pinch of salt into a bowl. Add the butter and rub into the flour until the mixture resembles fine breadcrumbs. Add about 2 tbsp ice-cold water and stir it in, then use your hands to bring the mixture together and knead it gently into a ball of dough. You can also do this stage in a food processor, adding the water then whizzing it in. Just tip the mixture into a bowl and bring together with your hands as before. Wrap and chill for 15 minutes.

2 Roll out the pastry thinly and line a loose-bottomed 21cm, deep fluted tart tin. Chill for around 15 minutes.

3 Preheat the oven to 200°C/180°C fan oven/gas mark 6. Line the pastry case with greaseproof paper and baking beans and bake blind for 10-15 minutes or until the pastry feels just dry. Remove the paper and beans and return to the oven for a couple more minutes until completely dry to the touch. Reduce the heat to 180°C/160°C fan oven/gas mark 4.

4 Heat the oil in a frying pan and gently fry the spring onions and thyme leaves until softened and beginning to colour. Add in the spinach, then season and stir until just wilted. Remove from the heat. In a bowl, whisk the crème fraîche with the eggs and season well.

5 Arrange the onion and spinach in the base of the tart. Pour over the egg mixture. Spoon little dollops of the cheese evenly over the top. Bake for 25-30 minutes or until just set.

6 Turn out and serve warm or cool with a crisp salad.

"If you have any nutmeg in the cupboard, add a good grating to the spinach as it wilts in the pan."

Chicken satay with spicy peanut sauce

This Asian-style starter is a Thai stalwart, but preparing it at home is like falling off a log. Make sure you soak the wooden skewers well to stop them burning. If you like it hot, turn up the heat with chilli powder in the dip.

prep 15 mins, plus marinating cook 15 mins SERVES 4

ingredients

For the chicken

8 wooden skewers
6 tbsp olive oil
Juice of 1 lime
1-2 garlic cloves, sliced
1 red chilli, deseeded and chopped
2 tbsp soy sauce
Salt and freshly ground black pepper
500g skinned, boneless chicken breast, cut into 2.5cm pieces
Fresh coriander leaves and wedges of lime, to garnish

For the peanut sauce

200ml coconut milk
1 garlic clove, crushed
2.5cm piece root ginger, finely grated
½ tsp chilli powder
1 tsp ground cumin
1 tsp ground coriander
100g smooth peanut butter
50g salted peanuts, finely chopped
Chilli sauce, to drizzle

1 Soak the wooden skewers in a bowl of cold water.

2 Put the oil, lime juice, garlic, chilli and soy sauce in a shallow non-metallic bowl. Season well. Add the chopped chicken and toss to coat. Cover and chill for up to 1 hour.

3 To make the peanut sauce, put the coconut milk into a non-stick saucepan and slowly bring to the boil, stirring. Take off the heat, then gradually stir in the remaining ingredients, except the chilli sauce. Spoon into a bowl, drizzle with the chilli sauce, and set aside.

4 Preheat the grill, then thread the chicken evenly between the skewers. Place on a baking sheet and cook for 5-7 minutes, turning frequently. The chicken should be golden brown, and you know that it's cooked when the juices run clear when pierced with a knife.

5 Arrange the chicken on a plate with the lime and coriander leaves and serve the peanut sauce alongside.

"Freeze leftover coconut milk in an airtight container for up to one month."

Smoked trout, potato and caper salad

Here's an anytime, throw-together bowl of goodness, great for a midweek supper or an easy weekend lunch. For added oomph, spoon a dollop of soured cream on top of each bowl just before serving, with some freshly ground black pepper.

prep 15 mins cook 10 mins SERVES 4

ingredients

450g baby new potatoes
150g streaky bacon, diced
2 tbsp cider vinegar
4-6 tbsp olive oil
Salt and freshly ground black
    pepper
2 tbsp capers, drained
2 celery sticks, trimmed and
    finely sliced
200g smoked trout fillets,
    broken into pieces
1 avocado, stoned and chopped
Handful of cherry tomatoes,
    halved
2 tbsp mint leaves, freshly
    chopped

1 Bring a pan of lightly salted water to the boil, halve the potatoes and cook for 8-10 minutes until just tender but not soft. Drain well and refresh under cold water. Transfer to a salad bowl.

2 Meanwhile, cook the chopped bacon in a dry frying pan (no need to add any oil as there's enough fat in the rashers).

3 Mix together the cider vinegar and olive oil in a small bowl to make a dressing, and season to taste.

4 Add the capers, celery, smoked trout pieces, avocado and cherry tomatoes to the potatoes. Drizzle over the dressing, then gently mix everything together and scatter over the mint at the end.

Potato Gorgonzola pizza

Okay, a potato-topped pizza may be a double dose of carbs, but this recipe is absolutely fantastic. You need to slice the potatoes really thinly to get them to cook until tender, so use a mandolin if you have one, or carefully pare the slices with a very sharp knife.

prep 15 mins cook 25 mins SERVES 2-4

ingredients

For the dough
250g strong bread flour
½ teaspoon dried yeast
1 tsp salt
½ tbsp olive oil

For the topping
3-4 tbsp pesto sauce (or see page 150 for recipe)
180g medium round potatoes, unpeeled
1 red onion, thinly sliced
1 tbsp rosemary sprigs
75g Gorgonzola cheese, crumbled
Salt and freshly ground black pepper
Extra virgin olive oil, to drizzle

1 Preheat the oven to 220°C/200°C fan oven/gas mark 7. Put a large baking sheet in the oven to preheat.

2 Sift the flour into a large bowl. Put the yeast in a small bowl and add 75ml water. Stir and set aside for 5 minutes to activate. Make a well in the centre of the flour and pour in the yeast mixture, 100-150ml water, the salt and the oil. Mix well to make a soft dough.

3 Roll out the dough on a sheet of lightly floured greaseproof or baking paper, to a circle of about 30-35cm. Transfer to the preheated baking sheet and spread with the pesto sauce.

4 Using a mandolin or really sharp knife, slice the potatoes very thinly. Scatter the slices over to cover the base.

5 Sprinkle with the onion, rosemary, cheese, seasoning and a little oil. Bake for about 15 minutes in the middle of the oven covered with foil. Remove the foil for a further 10-15 minutes to cook through, crisp up and brown off slightly.

Chicken and spicy arrabbiata sauce with pasta

Italian cooking is fast, fresh and flavoursome, and for this recipe you can add 'furious', too, because that's what 'arrabbiata' means – it's a reference to the heat from the chillies. This is healthy comfort food with a kick.

prep 10 mins cook 15 mins SERVES 4

ingredients

3-4 tbsp light olive oil
1 large onion, finely chopped
4 garlic cloves, chopped
400g can chopped tomatoes
100ml red wine
150ml hot chicken stock
1-2 red chillies, deseeded and
  finely sliced or chopped
1 tsp dried thyme
Salt and freshly ground black
  pepper
200g mushrooms, such as
  chestnut, quartered
350g skinless, boneless
  chicken, cut into strips
400g pasta, such as farfalle,
  penne or rigatoni
Fresh basil and Parmesan
  cheese, to serve

1 Pour the oil into a medium pan and heat gently. Add the onion and cook for around 15 minutes until softened. Stir in the garlic and cook for 1 minute.

2 Pour the chopped tomatoes into the pan with the wine and stock, then add the chillies and thyme. Season well. Bring to a gentle simmer and cook for about 5 minutes.

3 Add the quartered mushrooms and cook for a further 5 minutes or until the sauce is slightly reduced and thickened.

4 Season to taste and stir in the pieces of chicken. Cook over a gentle heat for 5-7 minutes until cooked through.

5 Meanwhile, cook the pasta in a big pan of boiling salted water, following the timings on the pack. Drain well into a large serving bowl. Pour over the tomato and chicken sauce, toss together and serve with basil leaves and a good sprinkling of grated Parmesan cheese.

"This dish is even quicker if you have leftover roast chicken to use up. Make up to Step 3, then add the chicken and cook for 2-3 minutes until heated through."

Posh lamb stew

The French give this wonderful meat and vegetable recipe the cheffy name of 'navarin' of lamb. It's a one-pot dish that takes long, slow cooking, resulting in melt-in-the-mouth, succulent meat in an aromatic and richly flavoured broth.

prep 15 mins **cook** 1½ hours **SERVES 4–6**

ingredients

900g boneless leg of lamb
Salt and freshly ground black
    pepper
50g unsalted butter
6 small onions, peeled and
    halved
3 celery sticks, sliced
1 tbsp plain flour
150ml medium dry white wine
150ml fresh lamb or beef stock
½ can chopped tomatoes
1 tbsp tomato purée
1 tbsp ground paprika
2 garlic cloves, crushed
1 bouquet garni
150g small carrots
150g small turnips
150g small potatoes
150g fine asparagus
1 tbsp coriander, roughly
    chopped

1 Cut the lamb into large cubes and season all over. Melt the butter in a non-stick pan and brown the meat, in batches, on all sides. Transfer to a bowl.

2 Add the onions and celery to the fat left in the pan and cook over a low-to-medium heat until beginning to soften. Stir in the flour and cook for 2-3 minutes until golden. Add the white wine and stock, chopped tomatoes and tomato purée, paprika, garlic and bouquet garni and bring to the boil, stirring continually to incorporate the sticky bits at the bottom into the mixture.

3 Return the lamb to the pan, cover tightly and cook over a gentle heat for about 1 hour, or until the meat is really tender. Every now and then, check there's enough liquid in the pan, and top up accordingly. Add the carrots, turnips and potatoes and continue to cook for 20 minutes until they are done, then add the asparagus and simmer for another 5 minutes or so until tender.

4 When ready to serve, check the seasoning, remove the bouquet garni, and sprinkle with fresh coriander.

"Although this is traditionally made in spring with young lamb and whole young spring vegetables, it can be made any time using older lamb. Just allow longer cooking time to ensure it's really tender."

TOP TIP

Don't mess with tender young carrots – eat them raw. Cut them into crudités with a vegetable peeler and serve with satay sauce or hummus.

MORE SPRING MAINS ▶

Roast duck with orange and caramelised shallots

Whole ducks are neat in size, less fleshy than chickens, and they have fantastic flavour. The richness is a perfect match for citrus and sour or dried fruits, so this recipe would be just as good with dried cranberries or sour cherries in place of the sweet raisins used below.

prep 10 mins cook 1¾ hours SERVES 4

ingredients

1 large duck weighing around
    1.75-2.25kg
12-14 shallots
A few sage leaves
1 tbsp olive oil
Salt and freshly ground black
    pepper
Zest and juice of 2 oranges
2 tbsp caster sugar
2 tbsp raisins
3-4 tbsp Cointreau
Watercress, to garnish

1 Preheat the oven 200°C/180°C fan oven/gas mark 6. Rinse the duck and wipe dry, then gently prick the skin all over with a fine skewer. Place 2-3 shallots and some sage leaves inside the duck. Rub all over with olive oil and salt and place on a trivet in a large roasting tin.

2 Roast the duck for 1½-1¾ hours, basting occasionally with fat. Drain and reserve the fat in the tin halfway through cooking.

3 Meanwhile spoon 1 tbsp of the duck fat into a frying pan and sauté the shallots until golden and nearly tender.

4 Add the orange zest and juice, sugar and raisins to the pan. Simmer gently until the liquid begins to thicken, and baste a little over the duck.

5 Check the duck is cooked through and the juices do not run pink. Turn the oven off and baste once again with a few spoonfuls of the orange sauce. Transfer to a warm serving dish, cover with foil and leave to rest for 10 minutes.

6 Add the Cointreau to the sauce and carefully light with a match, then close off the flames with a lid. Simmer until slightly reduced. Check the seasoning and pour over the duck. Garnish with watercress, and serve with roast potatoes and vegetables.

"Nothing makes you lose the will to live faster than having to peel a load of shallots - the multi-layered, papery outer skins are a nightmare to remove. Make it easier by covering them with boiling water in a bowl. Leave for 5 minutes, drain, and the water-soaked skins will slip off easily."

Seafood stew with king prawns, clams and sea bass

This rich and colourful collection of seafood is a sight to behold. The flavour comes from allowing the onion, chorizo and potatoes to first caramelise, then the fish is popped on top at the very last minute to steam, so it stays wonderfully moist.

prep 10 mins cook 25 mins SERVES 4

ingredients

2 tbsp olive oil
1 small red onion, chopped
2 garlic cloves, sliced
225g chorizo, sliced or chopped
300g new potatoes, chopped
1-2 sprigs of thyme
400g can chopped tomatoes
125ml dry white wine
300ml hot fish stock
Salt and freshly ground black
    pepper
200g clams
200g whole prawns
400g sea bass, cut into chunks

1 Heat the oil in a pan and sauté the red onion for 10 minutes until softened. Stir in the garlic and chorizo and continue to cook for 5 minutes. Add the new potatoes and thyme, cover the pan and cook over a low-to-medium heat for another 5 minutes. Shake the pan every now and then to make sure the potatoes aren't sticking.

2 Pour the chopped tomatoes, wine and fish stock into the pan. Season well. Bring to the boil and bubble for a couple of minutes to cook off the alcohol.

3 Stir in the fish: start with the clams, followed by the prawns. When the clams have opened and the prawns have turned from grey to almost pink, add the delicate pieces of sea bass on top, so that they steam in the heat of the sauce. Cook for a couple of minutes until the fish is translucent, then serve immediately.

"Serve with garlic and parsley croûtes. Mince a garlic clove and stir into a knob of softened butter with 1-2 tbsp freshly chopped parsley. Toast slices of baguette under a hot preheated grill, then spread with the butter. Return to the grill to melt the butter, warm through, and serve."

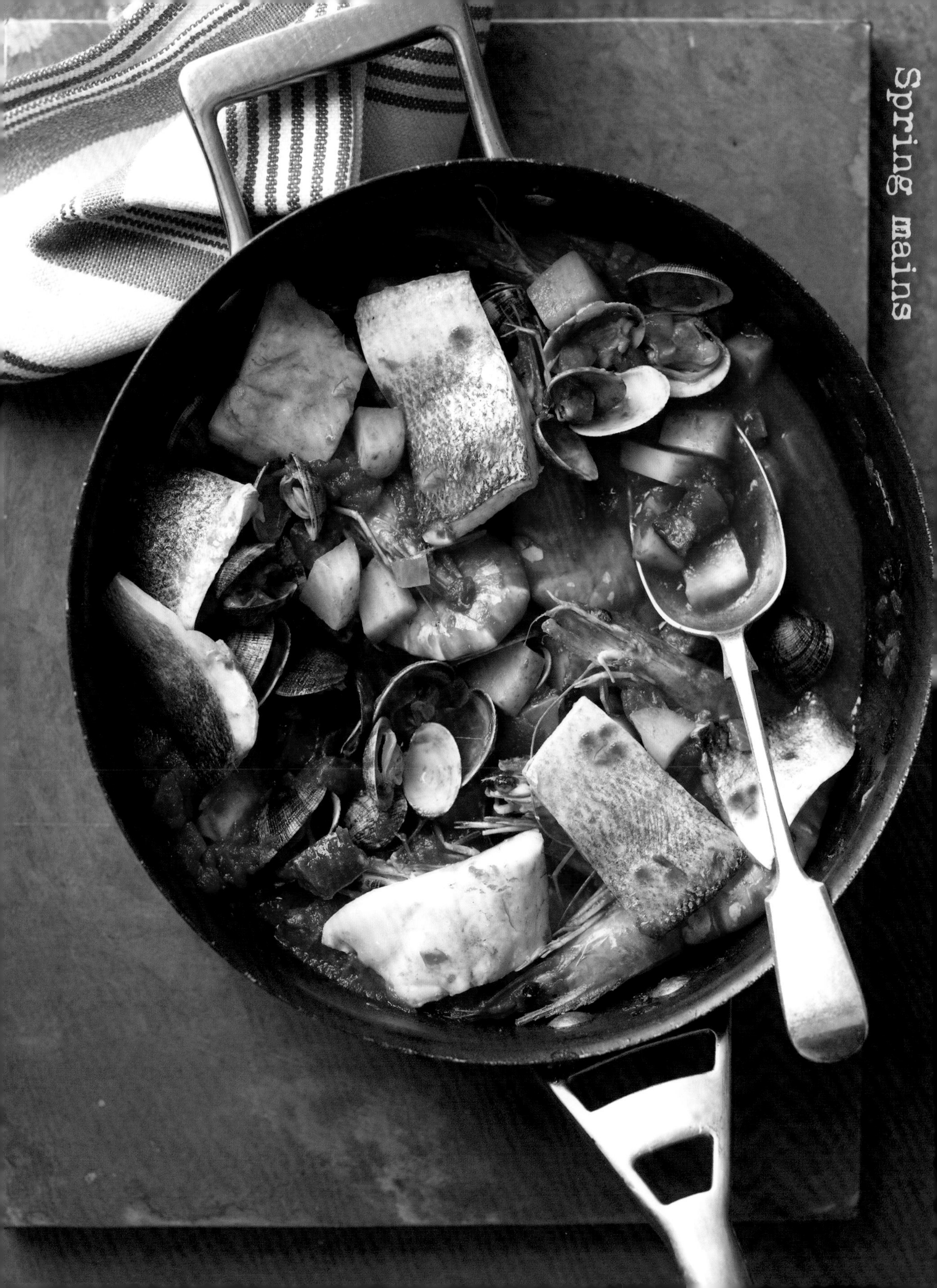

Poussins with a honey and lemon glaze

Here's a dish that could give anything served in the bistros of France a run for its money. It's quick to knock up and invariably gives stunning results. Those beautiful baby chickens known as 'poussins' have a deliciously sweet flavour and soft-textured meat. Give each guest one poussin with cook-in-the-oven pommes frites and a crisp green salad.

prep 10 mins, plus marinating cook 35-40 mins SERVES 4

ingredients

3 tbsp runny honey
Zest of 1 unwaxed lemon
Juice of 2 unwaxed lemons
1 tsp wholegrain mustard
1 garlic clove, crushed
4 tbsp olive oil
Salt and freshly ground black
    pepper
4 poussins
2 tbsp freshly chopped soft-
    leaved herbs, such as parsley,
    chervil, chives, mint or basil

To serve
Crisp green salad and easy
    pommes frites (see tip below)

1 In a bowl, mix together the honey, lemon zest and juice, mustard, garlic and olive oil. Season the poussins inside and out with the salt and pepper, then put them into an ovenproof dish. Pour the glaze all over them, then cover and set aside to marinate for 30 minutes. Preheat the oven to 200°C/180°C fan oven/gas mark 6.

2 Uncover the poussins and transfer to the oven. Roast for 35-40 minutes, depending on size, basting with the glaze halfway through cooking. Check the poussins are cooked by piercing the thigh (the thickest part of the bird) to see if the juices run clear. If they're pink, continue to cook at 5-minute intervals.

3 Cover the dish with foil and set aside to rest for 10-15 minutes. Stir the herbs into the juices, check the seasoning again and serve.

"For easy pommes frites, cut 4 medium potatoes into matchsticks the length of your middle finger. Toss in a bowl with a little olive oil and season well with salt. Tip onto a baking sheet lined with baking parchment and, halfway through cooking the chicken, roast in the oven at 200°C/180°C fan oven/gas mark 6 for 20 minutes. When the chicken comes out of the oven, continue to cook for another 10 minutes."

Italian-style saucy spare ribs

Braising spare ribs over a long, slow heat until they're falling off the bone makes a deliciously tender and heartwarming dish. Or try our tip below to turn them into another equally terrific meal.

prep 15mins cook 3 hours 15 mins SERVES 4

ingredients

1kg rack of loin ribs
2 tbsp sunflower or grapeseed
  oil
1 onion, chopped
3 large garlic cloves, crushed
227g can chopped tomatoes
3 tbsp tomato ketchup
2 bay leaves
500ml beef stock
100ml red wine
75ml Fernet Branca
2 tbsp Worcestershire sauce
Salt and freshly ground black
  pepper

1 Cut the long racks into three or four pieces (each piece will consist of three or four ribs). Heat half the oil in a large saucepan and brown the pieces or ribs for a couple of minutes on each side. Transfer to a plate.

2 Add the remaining oil to the pan and sauté the onion for 10 minutes until starting to soften. Stir in the garlic and cook for 1-2 minutes. Add the chopped tomatoes, ketchup, bay leaves, stock, red wine, Fernet Branca and Worcestershire sauce. Season well. Bring to the boil and cook for a couple of minutes.

3 Add the ribs to the liquid, cover with a lid and reduce the heat to a simmer. Cook for 3 hours until the meat is very tender and starting to come away from the bone.

4 Remove the ribs from the sauce and keep warm. Leave the pan on the heat and bring to the boil. Simmer for 10-15 minutes until the sauce has reduced by about half.

5 Return the ribs to the sauce to heat through, then spoon onto plates and let everyone dig in.

"In the unlikely event that there are leftovers, take the meat off the ribs, shred it, then stir it into any remaining sauce. Heat it up and serve tossed through tagliatelle pasta with lots of fresh parsley and grated Parmesan cheese."

Simple saltimbocca

This traditional Roman dish means 'jump in the mouth', as in 'I didn't eat all of them, honest – they just jumped into my mouth'. It's usually made with veal escalopes, but pork and turkey work just as well.

prep 10 mins cook 15 mins SERVES 4

ingredients

4 x 150g veal fillets
Salt and freshly ground black
    pepper
1 lemon
4 slices Parma ham
A few fresh sage leaves
1 tbsp plain flour
30g butter
2-3 tbsp light oil
7-8 tbsp dry white wine and
    stock mixed

1 Place a fillet between two sheets of greaseproof paper and flatten it with a rolling pin – you're aiming to get it to about twice the size and half the thickness. Now repeat for the remaining fillets.

2 Season on both sides with salt and black pepper and a grating of lemon zest.

3 Wrap a slice of ham around each fillet, then top with a sage leaf. Cut 4 slices from the lemon and secure one to each fillet with a cocktail stick. Coat lightly with the flour.

4 Heat the butter and oil in a close-fitting, heavy-based frying pan and, when bubbling, add the fillets. Cook over a medium heat, turning once or twice until lightly and evenly browned on all sides. Don't worry if they shrink a little. Transfer to a heated dish and keep warm.

5 Meanwhile, stir the wine and stock into the pan juices and bring to bubbling. Cook briefly to reduce slightly. Return the fillets to the pan and baste with the juices.

6 Remove the cocktail sticks and serve with a little of the sauce, sprinkled with black pepper and chopped sage.

"Italian main courses are usually served very simply with just one vegetable such as wilted spinach, dressed peas or simple green beans. If you want to bulk it up, steam new potatoes to go with it."

Spicy kebabs with simple sides

Marinating the meat in lemon, yoghurt and spices both flavours and tenderises it. Traditionally, lamb is used in Indian cooking, but these kebabs are just as delicious with beef. Get the grill really hot before you start, so that they cook quickly and evenly, leaving the cubes just pink on the inside.

prep 25-30 mins cook 30 mins SERVES 4

ingredients

8 small wooden skewers
450g lamb leg steaks, or sirloin
    or rump steak
4 tbsp natural yoghurt
1 garlic clove, crushed
2 tsp ground coriander
½ tsp ground cinnamon
½ tsp ground turmeric
1 tsp chilli powder or hot
    paprika
Juice of ½ lemon
1 tbsp olive oil
Lemon wedges, to serve

For the sides
¼ cucumber, deseeded and
    finely chopped
150g natural yoghurt
Pinch of ground cumin
1 tsp white wine vinegar
100g cherry tomatoes, halved
½ bunch radishes, chopped
2 spring onions, finely chopped
Olive oil
Coriander, to garnish
Salt and freshly ground black
    pepper

1 Soak the wooden skewers in a bowl of cold water. Trim any fat off the meat and cut into 2cm cubes.

2 Mix the yoghurt, garlic, spices, lemon juice and oil in a bowl. Add the meat and massage the yoghurt marinade into it briefly. Cover and chill for at least 1 hour, and up to 8 hours.

3 Prepare the sides. Mix together the cucumber, yoghurt, cumin and white wine vinegar. Season well. Toss the tomatoes, radishes and spring onions in a little olive oil and seasoning. Set both salads aside until ready to serve.

4 When ready to cook, preheat the grill to hot. Thread the meat onto the skewers, then cook for 4-5 minutes each side, depending on how pink you like your meat.

5 Serve with the sides, garnished with coriander and a wedge of lemon to squeeze over.

"To turn this dish into a main course, serve over basmati rice, or stuff into a naan bread, drizzle with the yoghurt and cucumber sauce, and spoon the salad on top."

Lamb boulangère

This is a classic, super-easy way to serve lamb for the Easter feast (or any time you fancy). The name comes from an old French village tradition in the days before people had ovens, when they'd take their roasts to the local bakery to cook them in theirs after the loaves were done. It produces its own wonderful juices, but if you want to serve it with gravy, see the tip below.

prep 20 mins cook 2 hours SERVES 6-8

ingredients

3 ½-4kg leg of lamb
A few sprigs of rosemary
2 cloves garlic, sliced
Salt and freshly ground black
   pepper
2 tbsp olive oil
Knob of butter
1 large onion, sliced
900g small potatoes, just
   scrubbed or peeled if you wish
300ml beef or lamb stock

1 Preheat the oven to 170°C/150°C fan oven/gas mark 3. Put the leg of lamb on a board and, using a sharp knife at a slight angle, puncture it all over. Push a small sprig of rosemary and slice of garlic into each puncture point. Season well.

2 Heat the oil and butter in a large pan and cook the onion quickly, along with any remaining garlic, until just softened. Transfer to a roasting tin with the potatoes, seasoning, and a few more sprigs of rosemary.

3 Lay the lamb on top, then pour over the stock, cover with foil and cook for about 2 hours, basting occasionally. If you like, remove the cover for the last 15 minutes or so to crisp up the meat or potatoes.

4 Slice and serve with the potatoes and steamed vegetables.

"Drain off the juices into a saucepan and place over a medium heat. Add a small glass of red wine and a spoonful of redcurrant jelly. Bring to the boil and simmer for a couple of minutes to burn off the alcohol. Mix 1 tsp cornflour with 2 tbsp cold water and stir in. Simmer until syrupy, then season to taste. Serve it in a jug alongside the lamb."

Spring side dishes that go with everything

Boiled, steamed, sautéed or stir-fried, these simple vegetable side dishes will add a punch to roasts, pan-fried fish, meat, griddled cheese or a terrific tart.

Leeks roasted with Parma ham

Cut four leeks in half or into three pieces. Drizzle with 1 tbsp olive oil, pour over 50ml white wine and season. Cover with foil and roast for 20 minutes in an oven preheated to 200°C/180°C fan oven/ gas mark 6. Uncover and check if the leeks are tender. Roughly scatter over the Parma ham and return to the oven for 10 minutes until crisp.

ⓥ Spiced cauliflower with cumin

Break 1 cauliflower head into florets. Heat 2 tbsp vegetable oil in a wok and stir-fry 2 finely sliced shallots until golden. Stir in 1 finely chopped green chilli, a 2.5cm piece root ginger cut into slivers, and 1 tsp cumin seeds. Add the cauliflower florets to the pan, season, and stir-fry for a few minutes until the cauliflower starts to caramelise. Pour in 200ml stock, cover, and continue to cook over a medium heat for 5 minutes or so until the veg is tender. Add a squeeze of lemon and serve with soured cream.

Spring greens with anchovy butter

Put 40g softened butter in a bowl and beat in the zest of 1 lemon, 1 deseeded and chopped red chilli, and 4 chopped anchovies. Chop 300g spring greens, removing woody stalks, and steam in a little water until just tender. Add the butter and toss to coat.

V New potato, watercress and spring onion salad

Halve or quarter 500g new potatoes, then simmer in a pan of boiling salted water for 15 minutes until just tender. Drain well. Chop a bunch of spring onions and sauté in a pan with a knob of butter and a drizzle of olive oil until just golden. Season well. Put the potatoes into a bowl and spoon the spring onions on top. Add the juice of half a lemon to the pan that cooked the onions with 2 tbsp extra virgin olive oil. Season well and heat gently. Pour over the potatoes and onions, then add a couple of big handfuls of watercress and toss everything together. Serve.

Hot cross buns

In Tudor times, people could eat hot cross buns only on Good Friday, Christmas and at burials, as the buns were reckoned to have supernatural powers and were hung on beams to protect households from evil spirits. But these days, we can eat them slathered with butter whenever we feel like a comforting treat.

prep 30 mins cook 1½ hours MAKES 12 BUNS

ingredients

For the buns
500g plain flour
1 tsp salt
1 tsp mixed spice
½ tsp ground nutmeg
50g sugar
50g butter, plus extra to grease
7g sachet easy blend yeast
110g raisins
25g finely chopped candied peel

For the crosses and glaze
A little beaten egg or milk
2 tbsp sugar, plus a little extra
100g plain flour

1 Sift the flour, salt, mixed spice and nutmeg into a bowl. Stir in the sugar. Rub in the butter until there are no lumps, then stir in the yeast, raisins and candied peel.

2 Make a well in the middle and pour in about 300ml hand-hot water. Mix with a knife to make a rough dough, then start to bring this together with your hands. Knead on a board for 5-10 minutes until soft, smooth and springy. You can also do this stage in a freestanding mixer using a dough hook. Return to the bowl, cover and leave to rise for 30 minutes.

3 Lightly grease a baking sheet. Divide the dough into 12 pieces, shape them into buns and place them on the tray about a centimetre apart to allow room to spread. Set aside in a warm place for about 40 minutes to prove.

4 Preheat the oven to 200°C/180°C fan oven/ gas mark 6. Mix together the milk or egg and sugar and brush over the buns. Sift the flour into a small bowl and stir in about 8 tbsp water to make a thick paste. Spoon into a piping bag fitted with a 5mm nozzle. Pipe over the buns to make crosses.

5 Bake for 20-25 minutes until golden and just firm. Lightly tap the base of one – if it's done it'll sound hollow. Dissolve the sugar in a little warm water and brush over the hot buns. Transfer to a wire rack to cool before serving.

"For the crosses, instead of the flour and water paste you can also use about 25-50g shortcrust pastry rolled out on a board and cut into thin strips. Place them on top of the buns before baking."

SPRING PUDDINGS & BAKES

Rhubarb lollies

The sharp, tart taste of rhubarb cries out for a touch of spicy sweetness to soften it. Preserved stem ginger is the perfect partner to balance poached fruit. If you don't want to make lollies, ripple the poached fruit together with the custard and freeze to make ice cream instead.

prep 15 mins, plus freezing time cook 5 mins SERVES 6

ingredients

500g rhubarb
50g golden caster sugar, plus
    extra to sweeten
Juice of ¼ orange
2 balls stem ginger, drained of
    syrup, finely grated
2 tbsp stem ginger syrup
300ml fresh custard

1 Chop the rhubarb into small pieces and put in a pan. Add the sugar, orange juice, stem ginger and ginger syrup, cover and bring to the boil. Simmer for a couple of minutes until just tender and the rhubarb has softened. Cool. Taste the rhubarb to check whether it needs more sugar at this stage.

2 Spoon a little rhubarb into the bottom of six freezer-proof glasses. Freeze for half an hour until firm. Push a lolly stick into the bottom and continue to freeze until solid.

3 Spoon a layer of custard on top and freeze until almost frozen. Continue to layer up the custard and rhubarb combination, freezing at each stage until the ingredients are all used up. Freeze the lollies until they are solid.

4 Remove from the freezer about 10 mins before serving to allow the lollies to soften a little, then twist them out and serve.

Easiest-ever chocolate tart

Serve up this pud and soak up the praise. There's no cooking involved at all – just a bit of whizzing and simmering, with a dash of creative flair. The decoration looks super-professional, yet it's incredibly easy.

prep 25 mins, plus overnight chilling   SERVES 10-12

ingredients

For the base
75g butter, melted, plus extra
   to grease
120g digestive biscuits
100g amaretti biscuits

For the filling and decoration
350g dark chocolate, at least
   50% cocoa solids, broken into
   pieces
600ml double cream
50g icing sugar
3 tbsp Amaretto liqueur
A little vegetable oil
20g flaked almonds
100g granulated sugar

1 Grease and line a 23cm springform tin with baking parchment.

2 Make the base. Whiz the digestive and amaretti biscuits in a food processor to make fine crumbs. Tip into a bowl and stir in the butter. Spoon into the prepared tin and chill until firm.

3 Put the chocolate in a bowl resting over a pan of gently simmering water and allow it to slowly melt. Once melted, heat the cream in a pan with the icing sugar and liqueur until it just comes to the boil. Carefully fold it into the melted chocolate until smooth. Pour into the prepared tin on top of the biscuit base. Chill overnight.

4 About an hour before you're ready to serve, make the praline. Line a baking sheet with a piece of baking parchment. Brush it with oil, then scatter over the almonds.

5 Put the sugar in a heavy-based pan and place over a low heat to allow it to slowly dissolve. Continue to heat, shaking the pan every now and again so the sugar dissolves easily, until it has turned into caramel and is a dark toffee colour. Quickly pour the caramel over the almonds and ensure they're evenly covered. Allow to cool.

6 When ready to serve, carefully lift the tart out of the tin, peeling away the paper around the side and from the base (use a palette knife or fish slice for this bit). Transfer to a serving plate. Roughly break up the caramel into shards and arrange on top of the tart. Serve immediately.

Fresh elderflower cordial with ginger and lime

In days gone by, this was an asthma and hayfever treatment – now we drink it simply because it's delicious. From the end of May to early June, the elder tree sprouts plate-heads of fragrant white flowers. Pick them when they're dry, newly opened and still creamy white – once they go brown they lose their flavour. Store the cordial in the fridge and use it up within a couple of months.

prep 30-45 mins, plus overnight soaking cook 5-10 mins MAKES 1.5 LITRES

ingredients

50g citric acid
25-30 elderflower heads
Zest and juice of 2 limes
2.5cm fresh root ginger, grated
1.2kg granulated sugar

1 Sprinkle the citric acid into a bowl and add the elderflower heads.

2 Pour 750ml water into a pan and bring to the boil. When the water is boiling, add the lime zest, juice, ginger and sugar. Simmer for a couple of minutes, stirring all the time, to dissolve the sugar. Pour into the bowl with the elderflower heads, stir, then cover and set aside for 24 hours.

3 Line a sieve with clean muslin and rest over a large bowl or jug. Carefully ladle the syrup into the muslin and allow it to drain.

4 Use a funnel to decant the syrup into sterilised bottles or jars (see tip below) and store in the fridge.

To serve
Pour 1-2 tbsp syrup into a glass and top up with still or sparkling water.

"Sterilise bottles and jars by washing them in hot soapy water (either by hand or in the dishwasher) then put them in the sink and pour boiling water into them until it overflows. Pour the water out and fill with the syrup."

BEST IN SEASON

SUMMER

June

Asparagus (early in the month), broad beans, carrots, cauliflower, cherries (from Europe), elderflowers, gooseberries, Jersey Royal potatoes, lettuce, mushrooms (including wild St George's), parsnips, peas (including sugar snaps), radishes, rocket, sorrel, watercress

Wood pigeon

Black bream, crab, cuttlefish, freshwater crayfish, mackerel, pollock, river trout, sea bass, sea trout, wild salmon

July

Apricots, beetroot, blackcurrants, blueberries, broad beans, carrots, cauliflower, cherries (homegrown and from Europe), courgettes, French beans, globe artichokes, gooseberries, kale, kohlrabi, lettuce, mushrooms, (including wild chanterelles and chicken of the woods), onions, pak choi, peas (including sugar snaps), potatoes, radishes, raspberries, redcurrants, rhubarb (outdoor), runner beans, sorrel, spinach, strawberries, tomatoes, watercress, white currants

Rabbit, wood pigeon

Black bream, cuttlefish, freshwater crayfish, lobster, mackerel, pollock, river trout, sea bass, sea trout

August

Apples (early, such as Discovery), apricots, aubergines, beetroot, blackberries, blackcurrants, blueberries, broad beans, broccoli, cabbage (green), carrots, cauliflower, chard, courgettes, cucumber, fennel, French beans, garlic, globe artichokes, kohlrabi, lamb's lettuce, loganberries, mushrooms (including chanterelles, chicken of the woods, field, horse, oyster, parasol, puffballs, wild ceps/porcini), onions, pak choi, peas (including sugar snaps), plums, potatoes, radishes, raspberries, redcurrants, rocket, runner beans, salsify (and scorzonera), samphire, sorrel, spinach, sweetcorn, tomatoes, watercress, white currants

Grouse, rabbit, snipe, teal, widgeon, wild duck, wood pigeon

Black bream, freshwater crayfish, lobster, mackerel, pollock, prawns, river trout, scallops, sea bass, spider crab and brown crab

Summer

Starters

No-cook chilled gazpacho **V**	80
Prepare-ahead easy cheese soufflés **V**	82
Cherry tomato and onion tartlets **V**	86
Stuffed courgette flowers **V**	88
Salt-and-pepper squid	90

Mains

Cajun chicken	94
Tuna with a Provençal-style sauce	96
Easy paella	98
Simple pan-fried salmon with Asian-style cucumber sauce	100
Pan-fried chicken and puy lentil salad	102
Fillet of beef with herb butter	104
Warm crab salad	108
Pan-fried pork and mushroom pasta	110
Chorizo and potato tortilla	112
Italian-style shellfish with tagliatelle	114
Super-easy fish with a mustard and herb crust	116
Spicy lamb burgers	120
Pork in orange and ginger marinade	122
Summer side dishes that go with everything **V**	124

Puddings & bakes

Mini pavlovas	126
Mini apricot and raspberry puff pastry tarts	128
Lavender butter biscuits	130
Eton mess	132
Peach and almond tart	134
Ginger and apricot ripple ice cream	136
Strawberry trifle	138
Summer cordials	140

IDEAL MENU SUGGESTION

Cherry tomato and onion tartlets
A Mösel Riesling Spätlese (white) or a Rosso di Montalcino (Tuscan red) are perfect companions

Chicken and lentil salad
A Martinborough Pinot Noir (red) or a white Châteauneuf-du-Pape will augment the flavours of the salad nicely

Eton mess or mini pavlovas

ideal HOME SHOW
TRUSTED FOR OVER 100 YEARS

No-cook chilled gazpacho

This vegetable-rich soup from Spain's southern Andalusia is usually
served chilled in an attempt to relieve the searing heat of summer.
With just 15 minutes' prep and no cooking at all, it's perfect for life in
the fast lane. Now all we need is the weather…

prep 15 mins SERVES 6–8

ingredients

½ mild red onion, roughly chopped
½ each red and green pepper, deseeded
    and roughly chopped
900g plum tomatoes, roughly chopped
700ml tomato juice or passata
2 large garlic cloves
1 small cucumber, peeled and deseeded
1 thick slice of day-old bread, cut into
    chunks
6 tbsp olive oil, plus extra to serve
2 tbsp sherry vinegar
Tabasco, to taste
Salt and freshly ground black pepper

For the garnish
1 tbsp stoned black olives

1 Set aside 1 tbsp each of the red onion and peppers.
Put the tomatoes, tomato juice or passata, garlic,
cucumber, remaining onions and peppers and bread
in a food processor or blender. Blitz to make a
smooth soup.

2 Add the olive oil, vinegar and a dash or two of
Tabasco. Season to taste. Whiz again and check the
seasoning. Chill for at least 4 hours.

3 When ready to serve, finely chop the reserved onion,
peppers and olives. Divide the soup among bowls,
top with the garnish and serve with a slick of olive oil.

Prepare-ahead easy cheese soufflés

This is a very handy first course because you can start them ahead of time and finish them off when your guests are at the table – yes, you really do cook them twice. Don't panic when they sink on the first bake – all you do is drizzle them with cream and extra cheese, then cook them a second time. They'll still have that light, fluffy texture.

prep 30 mins cook 35 mins SERVES 6

ingredients

40g butter, plus extra for
    greasing
300ml milk
1 bay leaf
40g plain flour
150g mature Cheddar, grated
2 tsp Dijon mustard
A good grating of nutmeg
Salt and ground white pepper
3 medium eggs, separated
1 tbsp chives, freshly chopped
100ml double cream

To serve
Salad and cherry tomatoes

1 Preheat the oven to 200°C/180°C fan oven/gas mark 6. Butter six 150-200ml ramekins.

2 Pour the milk into a pan and add the bay leaf. Place over a medium heat and as soon as bubbles appear around the edge showing that it has just started to boil, remove from the heat. Discard the bay leaf.

3 Melt the butter in a pan and, with a wooden spoon, stir in the flour. Cook for 1 minute, then take the pan off the heat and slowly pour in the milk, whisking all the time. Return the pan to the heat and cook, stirring constantly, until the mixture is smooth and thick.

4 Slide the pan off the heat again and stir in 100g grated cheese, the mustard and nutmeg, and season well. Set aside to cool for 5 minutes and then beat in the egg yolks and chives.

5 Whisk the egg whites in a clean, grease-free bowl until stiff peaks form. Add a spoonful to the cheese sauce mixture and fold in, then fold in the remaining egg whites. Spoon into the prepared ramekins and place them in a roasting tin. Pour in enough boiling water to come halfway up the sides of the dishes and bake for 20 minutes. Lift out of the tin and cool.

6 Run a knife around the ramekins and turn each soufflé into a baking dish. Turn the oven up to 220°C/200°C fan oven/gas mark 7. Sprinkle over the remaining cheese and drizzle with a little cream. Season again and bake for 15 minutes. Serve with salad.

TRUSTED FOR
· ideal ·
HOME SHOW
OVER 100 YEARS

"To prepare ahead, make the
soufflés up to the end of Step 5.
Cool, cover and chill for up to
a day. Complete the recipe when
you're ready to serve.
For a punchier flavour, add 2 tsp
grainy mustard with the Dijon."

TOP TIP

Artichokes are fantastic steamed and served with sauce gribiche, made by whisking together hard-boiled egg yolks, mustard and grapeseed oil, then stirring in chopped gherkins, capers, parsley, chervil and tarragon.

TRUSTED FOR
· ideal ·
HOME SHOW
OVER 100 YEARS

MORE SUMMER STARTERS ▶

Cherry tomato and onion tartlets

Forget about special equipment for making pastry – a bowl, plus your hands to rub the butter into the flour, will do just fine. These mini tartlets make brilliant summer fare served warm and garnished with a sprig of basil.

prep 20 mins cook 20 mins SERVES 6

ingredients

For the pastry
225g plain flour, plus extra for rolling out
25g Parmesan, finely grated
2 tsp wholegrain mustard
100g butter

For the filling
25g butter
1 small onion, thinly sliced
175g cherry tomatoes
100g Brie
2 large eggs
300ml double cream
Salt and freshly ground black pepper
2 tbsp pine nuts

1 Sift the flour into a mixing bowl and stir in the Parmesan and mustard. Rub the butter into the flour until the mixture resembles fine breadcrumbs. Or, if you have one, do this bit in a food processor.

2 Stir in 3 tbsp cold water and mix in until it starts to form clumps. Using your hands, bring together all the bits and knead gently to make a soft dough. If you need more water, drizzle in 1 tbsp at a time, stirring until the ingredients come together. Shape the dough into a disc, then wrap it in greaseproof paper and chill for 15 minutes.

3 Roll out the dough on a lightly floured surface then use it to line six individual 10cm tartlet tins. Prick the bases all over with a fork, then chill while you prepare the filling.

4 Preheat the oven to 200°C/180°C fan oven/gas mark 6 and put a large baking sheet in the oven to preheat at the same time. Melt the butter in a pan over a low heat and sauté the onion, covered with a lid, for 15 minutes until softened. Set aside to cool a little.

5 Halve the cherry tomatoes and slice the Brie. Beat the eggs and cream together in a jug and season well. Divide the cooled onion beween the tartlet tins, then add the tomatoes and Brie slices. Divide the filling evenly between each tin and scatter the pine nuts over the top. Bake on the preheated baking sheet for 20-25 minutes until just firm and golden. Serve warm or cold.

Stuffed courgette flowers

Along with English asparagus and broad beans, these are one of the few stunners that can only be enjoyed when they're in season. Look for the delicate female flowers that come attached to the courgette, and cook them straightaway.

prep 40 mins cook 15 mins SERVES 4

ingredients

200g ricotta, cream cheese or
    soft goat's cheese
3-4 tbsp finely grated Parmesan
2 tbsp finely chopped mixed
    herbs, such as basil, parsley,
    chervil and chives
1 tsp grated lemon zest
Salt and freshly ground black
    pepper
8-12 courgette flowers, with
    courgettes

For the salsa
1 ripe avocado, chopped
Squeeze of lemon juice
3 ripe plum tomatoes, peeled
    and chopped
2 spring onions, trimmed and
    finely chopped
Drizzle of chilli oil

1 Preheat the oven to 220°C/200°C fan oven/gas mark 7. Line a baking sheet with baking parchment.

2 Combine all the ingredients for the salsa together in a bowl, season well and set aside.

3 Mix together the ricotta and Parmesan, herbs, lemon zest and seasoning, and chilli. Carefully check over the flowers or wash and dry gently, if necessary, then with great care spoon a little of the mixture into each flower head. Put on the prepared baking sheet and drizzle with oil. Bake in the oven for 12-15 minutes until golden and the courgettes are just tender.

4 Serve with the salsa and an extra drizzle of chilli oil.

Salt-and-pepper squid

There are two cooking methods that turn out deliciously tender squid every time: either give it a quick flash in the pan, or braise it long and slow – anywhere in between and it'll be as tough as old boots.

prep 20 mins cook 50 mins SERVES 4

ingredients

Vegetable or sunflower oil, for deep-frying
500g fresh squid, prepared (see below)
2 tbsp rock or sea salt
2 tbsp roughly ground black peppercorns
1 tbsp roughly ground Szechuan peppercorns
Pinch of Chinese five spice
40g cornflour
1 large juicy lime, cut into wedges
Dipping sauce (see page 289), to serve

1 Fill a deep frying pan to one-third with oil, and place over a medium heat to heat through.

2 Prepare the squid as directed below (see tip). Open the body, then cut in half and use a knife to score a crisscross pattern all over it. Dry on kitchen paper.

3 Place the salt and peppercorns in a pestle and mortar, and pound until they are well cracked, but not finely ground. Place in a large bowl along with the Chinese five spice and cornflour, and shake well.

4 When the oil is hot enough (test with a crust of bread – it should brown within 1 minute) toss the prepared squid into the bowl. Remove a handful at a time, shaking off any excess flour. Cook in batches, lowering two pieces at a time gently into the hot oil. Line a large plate with kitchen paper.

5 Cook for about 1 minute or until they are just golden. Use a meal spoon to carefully separate pieces that have stuck to each other in the hot oil. Lift out of the pan with a slotted metal spoon, drain off excess oil, and then tip them onto the papered plate. Keep warm while cooking the rest in the same way.

6 Serve the squid with a wedge of lime and dipping sauce.

"To prepare squid, pull the head or tentacles away from the main body. Clean, then chop or slice the head. Inside the body are a black ink sac and a transparent, feather-shaped bone. Discard these, then peel off the pinkish outer skin. Discard this, too, and then rinse everything. Slice as directed, and drain on kitchen paper."

More celebrity chefs who cooked
at The Ideal Home Show

1

2

1) and 2) Italian chefs, **Gino D'Acampo** and **Aldo Zilli**. 3) Rugby player and foodie, **Matt Dawson**, won Celebrity MasterChef in 2006.
4) **Lily Simpson** is the founder of The Detox Kitchen.

SUMMER MAINS ▶

Cajun chicken

When the British deported the French-speaking Acadians ('Cajuns') from what is now Canada's Nova Scotia and New Brunswick, they also chucked out fantastic French rustic cooking. The Cajuns then took up residence in Louisiana, USA, and adapted it to the local ingredients. This recipe is a fine example, best served with rice, a crisp green salad, wedges of lemon and plenty of napkins.

prep 2 hours **cook** 50 mins **SERVES 6**

ingredients

12 small chicken wings or drumsticks
2 tbsp rum
2 tbsp soy sauce
2 tbsp lime juice
2 tbsp Cajun seasoning, or more to taste
2 tbsp olive oil
2 tsp sesame seeds (optional)
Wedges of lemon or lime, to serve

1 Place the chicken portions in a non-metallic dish, then use a sharp knife to slash each piece two or three times. Mix together the rum, soy sauce, lime juice and half the seasoning and rub well into the chicken, turning occasionally. Chill for 1-2 hours to marinate.

2 When ready to cook, preheat the oven to 190°C/170°C fan oven/gas mark 5. Take the chicken out of the fridge about 20 minutes before cooking, and transfer to a roasting tin along with any marinade from the dish. Cook for 40-50 minutes.

3 Halfway through cooking, sprinkle evenly and generously with the remaining seasoning and sesame seeds, and continue cooking until tender. Serve with wedges of lemon or lime.

"For a lean, low-fat version of this dish, use skinless chicken breasts and cook in the oven for 30-40 minutes until cooked all the way through."

Tuna with a Provençal-style sauce

Onions, tomatoes and black olives, cooked ultra simply, are typical of the Mediterranean, particularly the southern Provençal region of France. Don't overcook the tuna – like steak, it should still be pink in the middle for flavour and melt-in-the-mouth tenderness.

prep 10 mins cook 30 mins SERVES 4

ingredients

2 tbsp olive oil, plus extra for
   brushing
1 red onion, finely sliced
1-2 garlic cloves, finely sliced
300g vine ripened cherry
   tomatoes, halved
A few parsley stalks
2 tbsp sherry vinegar
4 x 150g tuna steaks
Black olives
A few basil leaves, to garnish
Salt and freshly ground black
   pepper

1 Heat the olive oil in a medium pan and sauté the onion and garlic for 10 minutes until starting to soften. Add the tomatoes and parsley stalks, plus about 150ml water and the sherry vinegar. Simmer gently for 10 minutes until the tomatoes have completely softened.

2 Put a frying pan or griddle over a medium heat until hot. Brush the tuna with olive oil, sprinkle with seasoning and then pan-fry for 2-3 minutes each side, or until cooked to your liking.

3 Stir the olives into the sauce and whip out and discard the parsley stalks. Season to taste. Divide the tuna among four plates and spoon over the sauce. Garnish with basil. Serve immediately with new potatoes and steamed green beans.

Easy paella

There are as many variations on this classic one-pot rice dish as there are cooks in Spain, but the principle is always the same: short, stubby paella rice cooked slowly in stock and seasoned with saffron, the king of spices. Utterly delicious.

prep 20 mins cook 50 mins SERVES 4

ingredients

A good pinch of saffron
200g fresh mussels, cleaned
    and scrubbed
2-3 tbsp olive oil
1 medium onion, chopped
2 garlic cloves, chopped
½ each red and green pepper,
    deseeded and chopped
200g tomatoes, skinned and
    chopped
400g paella rice
Salt and freshly ground black
    pepper
Zest and juice of 1 lemon
1 litre hot fish stock
4 small squid, cleaned and cut
    in rings
110g shelled peas
3-4 tbsp chopped parsley
110g prawns in shells
Wedges of lemon, to serve

1 Put the saffron in a bowl and add 100ml warm water. Set aside to infuse. Place the well-rinsed mussels in a large pan with a small glass of water. Cook for only a couple of minutes until the shells open, tossing occasionally. Discard any shells that don't open, then drain the liquid into a bowl.

2 In a very large frying pan or paella pan, heat the oil and fry the onion for about 15 minutes until translucent. Add the garlic, peppers and tomatoes. Cook for about 5 minutes, stirring occasionally. Add the rice and stir until well coated in oil, season and cook for 1-2 minutes.

3 Pour in the saffron liquid, lemon zest and juice, strained mussel liquid and 600ml of the stock. Bring to the boil, stirring once or twice, then cover very tightly with foil and a lid, and reduce the heat to the very minimum. Leave to cook, without stirring, for about 30 minutes (or place in the oven at 180°C/160°C fan oven/gas mark 4).

4 After about 30 minutes, stir in the squid, peas, half the parsley and extra stock as required. Cover well again and cook for a further 15-20 minutes (or longer in the oven), checking that it is not drying out. Add the prawns halfway through this stage.

5 Add the mussels in their shells, and sprinkle with the rest of the parsley. Allow the shellfish to heat through and serve with wedges of lemon.

"Paella can be cooked on the hob, on the barbecue, or in the oven, but whichever you choose, avoid stirring during the long, slow cooking, because all you're doing is letting the moist cooking steam and flavour escape."

Simple pan-fried salmon with Asian-style cucumber sauce

Fillets of fish cook in minutes and can be dressed up or down depending on what's to hand. An easy marinade gives the fish extra flavour, which then forms the base of a warm sauce to serve over the top with slices of crisp cucumber. This recipe works very well with tuna or cod, too.

prep 15 mins, plus marinating   cook 10 mins   SERVES 4

ingredients

4 x 150g salmon fillets, with skin
1 tbsp sesame oil
2 tbsp dry sherry
4 tbsp light soy sauce
1 tbsp lemon juice
2 spring onions, trimmed and
    finely sliced
1 red chilli, deseeded and finely
    chopped
2cm piece fresh root ginger,
    finely grated
½ cucumber
1 tbsp thick-set honey
1 tsp poppy seeds
Salt and freshly ground black
    pepper

1 Rub your fingers over the salmon to check for scales – scrape them off using a table knife against the skin, and discard. Rub the fish all over with sesame oil.

2 Mix the sherry, soy sauce, lemon juice, spring onions, chilli and ginger in a shallow dish. Add the salmon fillets and set aside for at least 15 minutes, or up to 2 hours.

3 Next, heat a dry frying pan until hot. Remove the fish from the marinade and cook, skin-side down, in the pan until crisp. Turn over and cook on the other side for 3-4 minutes until just cooked, but still moist inside.

4 Halve the cucumber lengthways. Scrape a teaspoon down the centre of each piece to remove the seeds, and slice into half-moon shapes.

5 Pour the marinade and honey into a small pan. Add the poppy seeds and bring to a gentle simmer. Add the cucumber and season well.

6 Place a salmon fillet on each plate, then spoon over the sauce, dividing the cucumber slices equally between them.

"You can cook the fish on the barbecue, too. Make the recipe up to the end of Step 2, then place on a preheated griddle or in a fish rack over the barbecue. Cook each side as per Step 3, turning whenever it begins to brown too much. Baste with a little of the marinade while it's cooking. The fish is ready when the flesh flakes easily when it's gently pierced with a sharp knife."

Pan-fried chicken and puy lentil salad

This is a brilliant midweek dish, but it's also special enough for a supper with friends. Preheat the pan before you cook the chicken (you should hear a sizzle as the meat hits it) to make the skin deliciously crisp and golden.

prep 20 mins cook 25 mins SERVES 4

ingredients

1 red pepper, deseeded and cut into quarters
3 large chicken breasts, with skin
2 thyme stalks, roughly chopped
1 tsp olive oil
Salt and freshly ground black pepper
175g puy lentils
1 small red onion, finely chopped
2 garlic cloves, crushed
500ml hot chicken stock
50g sundried tomatoes, halved
Handful of rocket

For the dressing
2 tbsp extra virgin olive oil
Zest and juice of ½ lemon

1 Preheat the grill. Put the pepper on a baking sheet and grill until the skins have blackened and blistered. Place in a bowl, cover and set aside while the skins steam off.

2 Put the chicken in a bowl and add the thyme and olive oil. Season well and toss together. Heat a large frying pan until hot and add the chicken, skin-side down, and cook until golden. Turn each piece over, cover with a lid and continue to cook over a medium heat until the chicken is cooked all the way through – around 15-20 minutes. Check that it is cooked by piercing the thickest part with a sharp knife. If the juices run clear, it's ready; if they're pink, let it carry on cooking until they run clear.

3 Put the puy lentils, red onion, garlic and chicken stock in a pan. Cover, bring to a gentle boil, then reduce the heat and simmer for around 20 minutes until cooked. The lentils should be tender, but still with a slight bite.

4 Peel the peppers and slice into strips.

5 Make the dressing. Remove the chicken from the pan and set aside on a plate. Return the pan to a low heat and add the extra virgin olive oil, lemon zest and juice and 2 tbsp water. Season and heat gently, stirring the base of the pan to mix in all the chicken juices. Pour any rested juices into the pan, too.

6 Spoon the lentils into a large bowl and stir in the sliced pepper, sundried tomatoes and hot dressing. Slice the chicken into thick pieces, arrange on top and scatter over the rocket. Serve.

"Cheat when you get to Step 3 by using ready-cooked puy lentils, and stir in some finely chopped spring onion in place of the red onion and garlic."

Fillet of beef with herb butter

For a special occasion, there's little to beat a luxurious fillet of beef that has been well hung to maximise the flavour. It's also super-lean, so slice it thickly and serve with herb butter, which turns into instant sauce as it melts. Choose the centre part (Chateaubriand) if possible for its even shape. Cooking time depends on thickness and preference.

prep 10 mins cook 35 mins SERVES 4-6

ingredients

Approx. 1kg piece from the centre of a fillet of well-hung beef
A few bay leaves
120g salted butter, at room temperature
1 tbsp freshly chopped herbs, such as chervil, chives, marjoram and parsley
A squeeze of lemon juice
Salt and freshly ground black pepper
Olive oil

1 Preheat the oven to 240°C/220°C fan oven/gas mark 9. Tie up the fillet evenly to keep a good shape during cooking, tucking in the occasional bay leaf as you go. Leave it to come to room temperature while you prepare the butter.

2 Blend 100g of the butter with the chopped herbs, lemon juice and seasoning until evenly mixed. Place on a sheet of greaseproof paper and wrap into a cylinder, tying up each end to give a long neat shape. Chill until required.

3 Heat the rest of the butter and the oil in a roasting tin until foaming. Add the beef and turn quickly in the hot fat to brown evenly all over. Transfer the tin immediately to the very hot oven and cook for about 20 minutes for rare, or up to 35 minutes for medium, turning it every 7-8 minutes.

4 When it's cooked to your liking, remove from the oven, cover with foil and leave to stand for 5 minutes. Heat a little herb butter in the roasting tin, stirring in any of the cooking juices, and then spoon this over the joint. Carve a thick slice for each person, and top each serving with more herb butter. Serve with new potatoes and steamed green vegetables.

"Go rustic and serve the fillet sliced on a wooden board instead of a plate, with a bowl of steaming, lightly buttered and seasoned new potatoes on the side."

TOP TIP

Steam runner beans, then drain and toss with olive oil, flaked almonds and a drizzle of good-quality balsamic vinegar.

MORE SUMMER MAINS ▶

Warm crab salad

This combination of crisp, crunchy vegetables, soft rice noodles and a punchy dressing with the delicate flavour of crab is pure paradise. If you like the brown meat, add it to the dressing to give it a creamy texture.

prep 20 mins SERVES 4

ingredients

For the salad
150g sugar snap peas, sliced
1 orange pepper, sliced
1 small red onion, finely sliced
1 ripe, firm mango, peeled and
    thinly sliced
1 red chilli, finely chopped
250-300g white crabmeat
250g rice noodles

For the dressing
4 tbsp mango dressing
Juice of ½ lemon
1-2 tbsp chilli oil
6 tbsp light olive oil
Salt and freshly ground black
    pepper

1 Mix together the sugar snaps, pepper, red onion, mango and red chilli, then gently flake in the crabmeat.

2 Mix all the dressing ingredients together in a bowl and season to taste.

3 Prepare the rice noodles according to the packet instructions. Drain and transfer to a bowl and stir in a little of the dressing straightaway.

4 Arrange the crab mixture on top. Pour on the rest of the dressing and stir through gently. Serve immediately.

"This salad is also delicious with pawpaw. Choose firm, just-ripe fruit for the best flavour and texture. (If it's over-ripe, it can taste too sweet and perfumed for a savoury recipe and the flesh may turn to mush.) You can find ready-made mango dressing easily, but you could just put a quarter of a mango in a blender with a drizzle of water and whiz until smooth."

Pan-fried pork and mushroom pasta

Pork fillet is lean, cooks quickly and is very tasty. Any shape of pasta works for this sauce, but you could also serve it on a bed of steaming long-grain rice.

prep 15 mins cook 25 mins SERVES 4

ingredients

1 tbsp olive oil

15g butter

1 small onion, finely chopped

1 garlic clove, crushed

1 pork fillet, around 350g, trimmed of any fat and sliced into 5mm pieces

100g button mushrooms, quartered

400g penne pasta

100g asparagus, each spear chopped into four

100g small courgettes, cut into 1-2cm thick slices

100ml white wine or stock

100ml chicken stock

Salt and freshly ground black pepper

2 tsp Dijon mustard

3-4 tbsp double cream or crème fraîche

Small bunch flat-leaf parsley, freshly chopped

1 Heat the oil and butter in a pan, and when the butter has melted add the onion. Cook gently for 10-15 minutes until softened. Stir in the garlic. Increase the heat and brown the pork all over. Add the mushrooms and stir over the heat for a few minutes until they begin to release their juices.

2 Cook the pasta in a large pan of boiling salted water, according to the timings on the pack. Drain, leaving a little water clinging to the pasta, then return to the pan.

3 Meanwhile, add the vegetables, the white wine and stock to the pork mixture. Season well, then simmer gently until the pork and vegetables are just cooked – around 3-5 minutes.

4 Tip the pork mixture into the pasta. Add the mustard to the meat pan, along with the cream, 2-3 tbsp chopped parsley and seasoning to taste. Bubble gently for a few minutes to thicken it slightly.

5 Spoon the pasta into four bowls, drizzle with sauce, and serve.

Chorizo and potato tortilla

Traditionally served as tapas, tortilla (or 'Spanish omelette', as it's known here) is a great dish for outdoors. It's just as good warm as it is cold, and if you're taking it on a picnic you can just slice it and serve it on chunks of bread, as the Spanish do.

prep 10 mins cook 10 mins SERVES 2-4

ingredients

2 tbsp olive oil
1 tbsp butter
1 chorizo sausage, diced
1 small red onion, chopped
1 small red pepper, deseeded
   and diced
4 cooked new potatoes, sliced
4 medium eggs
1 handful fresh basil and flat-
   leaf parsley, shredded
Salt and freshly ground black
   pepper

1 Heat the oil and butter together in an omelette pan, and when the butter has melted, add the chorizo, onion and red pepper. Cook gently together until the pepper and onion are soft and the chorizo is beginning to crisp. Add the new potatoes and stir everything together well.

2 Whisk the eggs with the herbs and plenty of seasoning just enough to break the eggs down, but don't overwhisk.

3 Pour the egg mixture into the pan and heat gently, pulling the cooked edges in towards the middle every now and again and spreading the uncooked egg out towards the rim of the pan.

4 Once the tortilla is set, place the pan under a hot grill for a couple of minutes to finish cooking the top – you want a nice golden crust. Garnish with basil and flat-leaf parsley. Serve immediately with a green salad.

"You can make this up to two days in advance, then store wrapped in cling film in the fridge."

Italian-style shellfish with tagliatelle

Use any selection of shellfish for this or stick to your favourites. Frozen scallops, mussels and prawns are all good substitutes if fresh fish isn't available, but make sure you first defrost thoroughly or the fish may toughen up on cooking.

prep 20 mins cook 12-15 mins SERVES 4

ingredients

500g fresh mussels, cleaned
    and scrubbed
2 tbsp olive oil
25g butter
4 spring onions, shredded
2 large garlic cloves, crushed
8 cherry tomatoes
8 small or 4 large scallops,
    removed from shells, rinsed
    and halved if large
175g prawns in shells
Salt and freshly ground black
    pepper
125ml dry white wine
400g dried tagliatelle
1 tbsp chopped parsley

1 Prepare the mussels, discarding any that are cracked or broken, and remove the hairy beard with a sharp knife. Rinse well. Heat half the oil in a large pan and add the mussels. Cover and cook briskly for 4-5 minutes, stirring frequently, until all the shells have opened. Discard any that refuse to open.

2 In a sauté pan heat the remaining oil with the butter until the butter starts to sizzle. Add the spring onions and garlic and stir over a high heat for a couple of minutes until the mixture softens, but before it browns. Turn the heat down to moderate and then add the tomatoes, mussels and their strained liquor, the scallops and prawns. Season well. Stir-fry for a minute or two to colour the scallops, then add the wine, bring to the boil and bubble briskly for 2-3 minutes.

3 Meanwhile, cook the tagliatelle in a large pan of boiling salted water according to the packet instructions until al dente (ever so slightly firm to the bite). Drain quickly, leaving a little water clinging to the pasta.

4 When the scallops are cooked (they should still be almost soft), toss the fish mixture with the tagliatelle. Season to taste and sprinkle with parsley.

"This delectable array of ingredients can be served as an appetising jumble on a plate. Alternatively, flick to page 323 and check out how to arrange pasta in an artistically controlled heap."

Super-easy fish with a mustard and herb crust

This no-effort dish is a great way to use up leftovers. A crust of bread, a chunk of Parmesan and a few sprigs of parsley together make a quick and crunchy topping for simple fish fillets.

prep 10 mins cook 20 mins SERVES 4

ingredients

3 tbsp olive oil, plus extra to drizzle
4 x 150g thick white fish fillets, such as cod or pollock
1 tbsp grainy mustard
Zest of 1 small orange
50g breadcrumbs
2 tbsp freshly chopped parsley
25g Parmesan, finely grated
Salt and freshly ground black pepper
4 sprigs cherry tomatoes on the vine

1 Preheat the oven to 200°C/180°C fan oven/gas mark 6. Lightly oil an ovenproof dish and arrange the fish in it. Mix together the mustard and 1 tbsp oil in a small bowl and brush evenly over the tops of the fish steaks.

2 Mix together the rest of the oil with the orange zest, breadcrumbs, parsley and cheese, and season well. Spread evenly over the fish, pressing down lightly so that it sticks to the fish. Put the tomatoes in a separate dish, drizzle with a little oil and season.

3 Bake the fish and the tomatoes in the oven for about 20 minutes, or until the fish is cooked through and gently flaking when pulled with a fork, and the topping is crispy. Serve with steamed vegetables and new potatoes.

"Ring the changes and serve the fish with a white bean mash instead of potatoes. Drain two cans of cannellini beans; put the beans in a pan with 200ml hot stock. Bring to a simmer and season. Mash well then stir in 1 tbsp extra virgin olive oil. Spoon on to plates and top with the fish and tomatoes."

TOP TIP

Parsley sauce has bags of flavour. Add fresh parsley to stocks or chop finely and stir through soaked bulgur wheat with chopped tomatoes, cucumber and red onion to make a tasty tabouleh.

MORE SUMMER MAINS ▶

Spicy lamb burgers

Anyone can make a good burger – all it takes is a pack of good-quality mince and any flavourings you have to hand. Just remember that onion needs to be grated, as it's not being cooked, but after that it's culinary freestyle all the way. Season the mixture well and check the seasoning by first frying off a teaspoonful to taste.

prep 15 mins cook 14 mins SERVES 4

ingredients

500g lean lamb mince
1 small onion, grated
1 small eating apple, grated
1 tsp ground cumin
½ tsp chilli flakes or 1 tbsp
   sweet chilli sauce
1 medium egg, beaten
50g fresh wholemeal
   breadcrumbs
Salt and freshly ground black
   pepper
1 tbsp sunflower oil
4 burger buns
2 tomatoes, thinly sliced
A handful of rocket

1 Place the lamb in a large mixing bowl and add the onion, apple, cumin, chilli (or chilli sauce), egg, breadcrumbs and seasoning.

2 Mix thoroughly with your hands until really well blended. Shape the mixture into four large burgers.

3 Brush each side of the burgers with a little oil and heat a frying pan until hot. Cook for 5-7 minutes per side, depending on how thick you've made the burgers. Serve them in burger buns with the tomatoes and rocket.

"Serve with potato wedges. Cut 4 large baking potatoes into wedges. Brush with oil and bake in a preheated oven at 200°C/180°C fan oven/gas mark 6 for approx. 40 minutes until golden."

"This mixture also makes great meatballs. Roll spoonfuls in your hands to make balls a bit bigger than a walnut. Fry off in a pan until golden and cooked through, then stuff into pitta bread with chopped salad and a drizzle of tzatziki."

Pork in orange and ginger marinade

This may be the quickest roast ever – and it's just as delicious cold. 'Nuff said.

prep 10 mins, plus marinating cook 30 mins SERVES 4

ingredients

Zest and juice of 1 large orange
2 tbsp orange marmalade
2cm piece fresh root ginger, grated
1 garlic clove, grated
2 tbsp maple syrup
Salt and freshly ground black pepper
500g pork fillet, trimmed of any skin or sinews
350g long grain and wild rice
200g baby leaf spinach
Knob of butter

1 Preheat the oven to 220°C/200°C fan oven/gas mark 7.

2 Mix together the orange zest, marmalade, ginger, garlic and 1 tbsp maple syrup, and season well. Rub all over the pork. Wrap in a parcel of foil and set aside for 15-30 minutes, if possible, then fast-roast for 15 minutes.

3 Cook the rice according to the packet instructions. Open out the foil on the pork and continue to roast for a further 10-15 minutes until lightly coloured.

4 Pour the orange juice, remaining maple syrup and roasting juices into a small pan and simmer until reduced by about half. Add seasoning to taste.

5 Wash the spinach well and put it in a pan with the butter over a low heat to wilt down. Season well.

6 Serve the pork thickly sliced on the mixed rice with the sauce and spinach.

"Spoon a mound of rice into the middle of the plate. Slice the pork on the diagonal and arrange three pieces on top. Drizzle the orange and maple sauce over, and serve with a tumble of just-wilted spinach."

Summer side dishes that go with everything

Boiled, steamed, sautéed or stir-fried, these simple vegetable side dishes will add a punch to roasts, pan-fried fish, meat, griddled cheese or a terrific tart.

V Braised Little Gem with peas and dill

Put 25g butter in a pan with ½ tbsp olive oil. Place over a medium heat. As soon as the butter has melted add 2 quartered Little Gem lettuces. Cook for 1-2 minutes to brown the lettuces. Add 100ml hot vegetable stock and 150g fresh peas. Cover and cook for 3-5 minutes. Transfer the vegetables to a plate. Take the pan off the heat and stir in 2 tbsp extra virgin olive oil and 2 tbsp soured cream, 2-3 tbsp freshly chopped dill, and season well. Swirl this dressing around the pan and pour over the lettuce and peas. Serve with a squeeze of lemon.

V Roasted tomatoes with garlic and basil

Cut 500g tomatoes in half through the middle (the ones on the vine have the most flavour), place on a baking tray and season well. Scatter 2 finely sliced garlic cloves over. Sprinkle with a little sugar and drizzle over 1 tbsp olive oil. Season well. Roast in the oven preheated at 200°C/180°C fan oven/ gas mark 6 for 20-30 minutes until tender. Transfer to a plate. Top with a handful of basil. Whisk 2 tbsp extra virgin olive oil and 1 tbsp red wine vinegar and season well. Drizzle over the top and serve.

Ⓥ Crisp fennel salad with lemon and Parmesan

Halve a small bulb of fennel and slice finely (if you have a mandolin, use it to make wafer-thin slices). Put in a bowl. Mix together 3 tbsp extra virgin olive oil and the juice of half a lemon. Season well and pour half over the fennel. Garnish with rocket and Parmesan shavings, and drizzle the remaining dressing over the top.

Ⓥ Sweet and sour peppers

Heat 2 tbsp olive oil in a pan and sauté 1 finely sliced onion for 10 minutes until the onion starts to soften. Stir in 2 sliced garlic cloves. Halve, deseed and slice 1 orange, 1 red and 1 yellow pepper, and add to the pan with 100ml dry white wine and 2 bay leaves. Season well. Bring to the boil and bubble hard for 2-3 minutes to cook off the alcohol. Cover the pan and reduce the heat. Cook for 50-60 minutes until the peppers have softened, periodically checking there's still liquid in the pan. Take off the lid and add 2 tbsp red wine vinegar and 1 tbsp capers. Bring to a bubble and simmer hard for 1-2 minutes until the liquid reduces and is syrupy. Serve.

Mini pavlovas

A crisp meringue base with a chewy filling, topped with whipped cream and a colourful selection of the season's fruit, is like waking up in paradise. What's more, the meringues can be made up to a week ahead – just store them in an airtight container in a cool place.

prep 25 mins cook 1 hour 5 mins SERVES 8

ingredients

4 large egg whites
Pinch of salt
225g caster sugar
½ tsp white wine vinegar
1 tsp cornflour
450ml double cream
1-2 tbsp elderflower cordial
   (see page 72)
Icing sugar, to sweeten and to
   dust
400g mixed summer berries
   (halve or quarter any large
   strawberries)

1 Preheat the oven to 180°C/160°C fan oven/gas mark 4. Line two baking sheets with baking parchment. Trace four 7.5cm rounds on top of each, then turn the paper over.

2 Whisk the egg whites in a spotlessly clean, grease-free bowl with a pinch of salt until the mixture is just stiff. You should be able to hold the bowl upside down without it moving. Gradually whisk in half the sugar and the vinegar, then fold in the rest of the sugar with the cornflour until the mixture is thick and glossy.

3 Dot a little meringue on the corner of each baking sheet to stick the parchment down. Spoon the meringue onto the traced rounds and make hollows in the centre of each one with a spoon.

4 Bake for 5 minutes in the centre of the oven, then reduce the heat to 130°C/110°C fan oven/gas mark 1. Carry on cooking for about 1 hour until the meringues are crisp, then let them cool.

5 Whip the cream until it forms soft peaks, then fold in the elderflower cordial with 1-2 tsp icing sugar to taste. Spoon this into the cold meringues, then top with the berries. Dust with icing sugar, then serve.

SUMMER PUDDINGS & BAKES

Mini apricot and raspberry puff pastry tarts

These terrific little sweet bites couldn't be easier: just roll out some puff pastry thinly, cut it into squares, and bake it with spiced fruit. Serve with a dollop of crème fraîche.

prep 20 mins, plus chilling cook 20-30 mins SERVES 6

ingredients

250g puff pastry
A little plain flour, for rolling out
1 egg, beaten
1 tbsp golden caster sugar, plus extra to dust
8 ripe apricots, stoned and quartered
½ tsp ground cinnamon
3 tbsp apricot jam, melted
250g raspberries
Knob of butter, melted
Crème fraîche and icing sugar, to serve

1. Roll the pastry, using a little plain flour, into a rectangle measuring 30 x 20cm approx. Transfer to a baking sheet, cover with clingfilm and chill for at least 1 hour or up to 24 hours.

2. Preheat the oven to 220°C/200°C fan oven/gas mark 7, and put in a baking sheet to heat up at the same time. Trim the pastry edges with a sharp knife. Cut into 6 rectangles.

3. Score a border using a sharp knife about 1cm inside the edge. Prick the middle all over with a fork. Return to the preheated baking sheet. Brush the edges with beaten egg and use half the sugar to sprinkle over the pastry tarts.

4. Put the apricots in a bowl and toss with the remaining sugar and cinnamon. Spoon onto the pastry tarts, and brush with a little melted apricot jam.

5. Bake for 15-20 minutes until the pastry is golden and puffed up. Reduce the oven temperature to 180°C/160°C fan oven/gas mark 4. Scatter over a few raspberries, brush with butter and return to the oven to bake for 5-10 more minutes until the pastry is golden.

6. Scatter over the remaining raspberries, sprinkle with icing sugar and serve with crème fraîche.

Lavender butter biscuits

This fragrant flower blooms from early to late summer. It's a real delicacy that works brilliantly in this biscuit recipe, especially when paired with an equally delicately scented fruit such as gooseberries (see tip).

prep 15 mins, plus chilling cook 12 mins MAKES 12 BISCUITS

ingredients

50g softened butter
40g caster sugar, plus extra to
    sprinkle
125g plain flour
1 tsp vanilla extract
2 tbsp milk
Lavender flowers

1 Preheat the oven to 190°C/170°C fan oven/gas mark 5. Line a couple of baking sheets with baking parchment.

2 Cream the butter and sugar together in a bowl using a wooden spoon or electric hand whisk.

3 Sift over the flour and pour over the vanilla extract and milk. Stir the flour in and then start to work the ingredients together to make a dough.

4 Roll out the dough on a lightly floured board until a couple of millimetres thick. Stamp into rounds using a 5cm cutter. Press a lavender flower in the middle. Chill for 15 minutes.

5 Transfer to the baking sheets and bake in the oven for around 12 minutes until just golden round the edges. Sprinkle with caster sugar, then transfer to a wire rack to cool completely.

"Serve with gooseberry fool. In an ovenproof dish, stir 75g caster sugar and 1-2 tbsp elderflower cordial (see page 72) into 600g gooseberries. Cook in an oven preheated to 180°C/160°C fan oven/gas mark 4 for 20 minutes or until really tender. Push through a sieve to extract the purée. Whip 300ml double cream until just thick, then fold into 300ml good-quality, ready-made custard. Fold the gooseberry puree into the cream mixture, then spoon into glasses and serve with the biscuits. Serves 6."

Eton mess

This has been served at the annual Eton v Winchester College cricket match since the 1930s. It's a terrific last-minute dessert, because no cooking is required: there's no point using anything other than ready-made meringues, as they just get crushed, and you can chuck in whatever fruits you fancy. Serve in tall, elegant glasses or lazily arranged in a large trifle dish.

prep 10 mins SERVES 6

ingredients

300ml double cream

A few drops vanilla extract

300ml thick Greek-style yoghurt (or add more cream if you prefer)

150g ready-made meringues, roughly broken up

250g ripe strawberries, raspberries or blackberries, or a mixture

Raspberry coulis (see tip below), to serve

1 Whip the cream in a bowl with a little vanilla until still soft and starting to thicken, then gently stir in the yoghurt to give a soft, spoonable consistency.

2 Add the crushed meringues and fruit to the bowl with the cream mixture and add a drizzle of the coulis. Gently fold everything together to mix – the result should be a tantalising-looking mess shot through with swirls of colour. Spoon into clear glasses and serve.

"For a quick raspberry coulis, mix 100g ripe raspberries with 1-2 tbsp caster sugar and press through a sieve to remove all the pips. Done."

Peach and almond tart

Fresh peaches are at their best in the middle of summer. Combine them with home-made marzipan and you'll think you've woken up in heaven. Choose peaches that are firm but just ripe. Too hard and they'll be difficult to slice, too soft and they'll turn to mush.

prep 20 mins, plus chilling cook 50 mins SERVES 8-10

ingredients

For the pastry
200g plain flour, plus extra for
   rolling out
1 tbsp golden caster sugar
100g chilled butter
1 medium egg yolk

For the filling
3-4 just-ripe peaches
75g butter
75g golden caster sugar
1 medium egg
75g ground almonds
½ tsp ground cardamom
2 tbsp self-raising flour
2 tbsp golden syrup
2 tsp rosewater

1 Sift the flour into a mixing bowl, add the sugar and rub in the butter until the mixture looks like fine breadcrumbs (or do this part in a food processor).

2 Whisk the egg yolk with 2 tbsp cold water and add to the bowl. Mix in using a round-bladed knife – it should look crumbly. Start to bring the mixture together with your hands to make a dough. If it feels dry, drizzle more water over and mix in. Knead the dough lightly until smooth, then wrap and chill in the fridge for 15 minutes.

3 Preheat the oven to 200°C/180°C fan oven/gas mark 6. Roll out the pastry on a lightly floured, clean work surface and use to line a 20cm loose-bottomed, fluted shallow tart tin. Prick the base all over and chill for another 15 minutes.

4 Line the pastry case with greaseproof paper or baking parchment, fill with baking beans and bake blind for 10-15 minutes until the pastry feels dry to the touch. Remove the beans and paper and set aside. Reduce the oven to 180°C/160°C fan over/gas mark 4.

5 Meanwhile halve (or quarter) the fruit and remove the stones. Slice thinly. Beat the butter and sugar in a bowl until pale and creamy. Gradually add the egg, little by little, then once it is all incorporated, fold in the ground almonds, cardamom and flour.

6 Spoon the mixture into the tart case and spread evenly over the base. Push the fruit into the mixture, then bake in the oven for 20-25 minutes until golden and cooked through.

7 Remove the tart from the oven. Heat the syrup and rosewater together in a small pan until the mixture is very runny. Transfer the tart to a serving platter and drizzle the syrup mixture over. Serve warm with cream or custard.

Ginger and apricot ripple ice cream

No need for any special ice-cream kit with this recipe – all it takes is a couple of bowls and an electric hand whisk (or a balloon whisk and plenty of elbow grease) to whip the air into the cream and egg whites and then fold everything together. The texture is softly creamy, yet frozen enough to hold its shape. (They'll think you're a genius!)

prep 30 mins, plus freezing cook 5 mins SERVES 6-8

ingredients

3 medium eggs, separated
250g golden caster sugar
1 tbsp ground ginger
1 tsp vanilla extract
600ml double cream
4 balls stem ginger in syrup,
   drained and finely chopped
2 tbsp ginger syrup from the jar
4 tbsp apricot preserve

1 Put the egg whites into a spotlessly clean, grease-free bowl and whisk with an electric hand whisk until soft peaks form. Set aside.

2 Put the sugar, ginger, vanilla and egg yolks into another bowl and whisk until thick and foamy – there's no need to wash the beaters between operations.

3 Pour the cream into a separate bowl and whip until just soft. Carefully fold into the egg yolk mixture. Add a spoonful of the beaten egg whites and fold in, then fold in the remainder. Pour into a freezer-proof dish. Freeze for 2 hours.

4 Fold in the stem ginger and freeze again for another 1-2 hours until almost firm.

5 Stir together the ginger syrup and apricot preserve, then press through a sieve into a bowl to make a smooth sauce. Drizzle over the ice cream and use a skewer to ripple through the mixture. Freeze until solid.

6 Scoop into balls and serve with wafers.

Strawberry trifle

Gone are the days when trifle meant jelly, sherry and soggy old sponge. This combination of fresh fruit, boozy make-it-yourself syrup and crisp sponge fingers is topped with ready-made fresh custard and softly whipped cream. Do sweeten the cream slightly, otherwise it can taste too savoury and cheesy against the other sweet ingredients. And take care not to overwhip – it should sit on top of the custard like a cloud.

prep 10 mins cook 5 mins SERVES 6-8

ingredients

Juice of 1 large orange
50g sugar
50ml Chambord liqueur
100ml red wine
450g strawberries, halved (leave little ones whole)
100g sponge fingers
600ml good-quality fresh custard
450ml double cream
1-2 tsp golden caster sugar

1 Pour the orange juice into a small pan and add the sugar, liqueur and red wine. Bring to the boil and simmer for 4-5 minutes until syrupy. Strain through a sieve and cool.

2 Set aside a third of the strawberries, then layer the remaining fruit in a bowl with the sponge fingers. Drizzle with half the syrup.

3 Spoon the custard on top. Whip the cream in a bowl until thick and mousse-like. Fold in the sugar.

4 Spoon the cream on top of the custard, then decorate with the reserved fruit.

5 Drizzle the remaining syrup over the top and serve immediately.

Summer cordials

Here's a delectable trio of thirst-quenchers. Serve one part cordial to five parts mixer (still, sparkling or soda water), and top with ice, a slice and a sprig of mint. A slug of gin or vodka would go down a treat, too. Alternatively, pour a measure of cordial into a flute and top with sparkling wine.

prep 10-20 mins cook 10 mins

ingredients

For the lemon zinger
500g granulated sugar • 250ml boiled water • Finely grated zest of 2 unwaxed lemons • Juice of 3 lemons
Makes around 500ml

For the raspberry fizz
250g granulated sugar • 250ml boiled water • 400g ripe raspberries • Squeeze of lemon juice
Makes around 400ml

For the tropical mango cooler
225g granulated sugar • 400ml boiled water • 200ml fresh lemon and orange or tangerine juice, mixed • 500g ripe mango pulp (the flesh from around 3 large mangoes)
Makes around 500ml

1 For each cordial recipe, put the sugar and water into a pan and heat gently, stirring occasionally, over a gentle heat until the sugar has dissolved.

2 Add the fruit and/or juice. Bring to the boil, then reduce the heat and simmer for 10 minutes.

3 Pour the cordial through a sieve lined with clean muslin into another large bowl.

4 Bottle in sterilised bottles and freeze or chill (see tips below).

"If you are freezing the cordial, use plastic bottles and allow at least 8-10cm headroom in the bottle for expansion during freezing. It will keep in the fridge for 3-4 weeks if well filtered, and the bottles are sterilised properly."

"To get the maximum juice from a lemon, roll firmly between your hands or over a clean firm work surface first."

"Use the lemon zinger recipe as the base for other citrus fruits - lime needs more sugar, while oranges and tangerines need less."

AUTUMN

BEST IN SEASON

AUTUMN

September

Apples (early and late), aubergines, beetroot, blackberries, blueberries, borlotti beans (fresh to pod), broccoli, cabbage (green), cauliflower, chard, courgettes, cucumber, damsons, fennel, French beans, globe artichokes, greengages, hazelnuts and cobnuts, kale, kohlrabi, loganberries, mushrooms (including chanterelles, chicken of the woods, field, horse, oyster, parasol, puffball, wild ceps/porcini), onions, pak choi, pears, peppers and chillies, plums, pumpkin, rocket, runner beans, salsify (and scorzonera), sorrel, squashes

Grouse, mallard, rabbit, wood pigeon

Black bream, eels, freshwater crayfish, lobster, mackerel, mussels, native oysters, prawns, river trout, scallops, sea bass, spider and brown crab, sprats, squid

October

Apples (late, such as Egremont Russet, and stored, such as Cox's), beetroot, borlotti beans (fresh to pod), broccoli, cabbage (green), carrots, cauliflower, celeriac, celery, chard, chillies, courgettes, fennel, kale, kohlrabi, leeks, medlars, mushrooms (including horse, oyster, parasol, puffballs, wild chanterelles, wood blewits), onions, pears, peppers, potatoes, pumpkins, quince, raspberries, rocket, salsify, spinach, squashes, tomatoes, turnips, walnuts

Grouse, hare, mallard, partridge, rabbit, snipe, wood pigeon

Cod, eels, lobster, mackerel, native and rock oysters, prawns, river trout, scallops, sea bass, spider and brown crab, sprats, squid, wild salmon

November

Apples (late and stored), beetroot, Brussels tops, cabbages (green, red and white), cauliflower, celeriac, celery, chard, chicory, endive, Jerusalem artichokes, kale, kohlrabi, leeks, lettuce, medlars, mushrooms (including oyster, wild horse, wood blewits), onions, parsnips, pears, potatoes, pumpkins, quince, raspberries, salsify and scorzonera, spring greens, squashes, swede, turnips, winter greens

Grouse, hare, mallard, partridge, rabbit, snipe, wood pigeon

Cod, crab, lobster, mackerel, mussels, native and rock oysters, prawns, scallops, sea bass, sprats, squid, whiting

Autumn

Starters

Roast pumpkin soup with dead-easy cheese straws Ⓥ	148
Surprise vegetable parcels Ⓥ	150
Posh coleslaw with Parma ham	152
Sweetcorn, coriander and cumin fritters with chilli jam Ⓥ	154
Pork crackling with apple sauce	156

Mains

Easy cod fish cakes with rocket sauce	160
Roast loin of pork	162
Corn on the cob with lime and coriander butter Ⓥ	164
Chicken and sausage cassoulet	166
Polenta with pesto and charred mixed peppers Ⓥ	170
Can't-go-wrong carrot and parsnip rosti Ⓥ	172
Beef and citrus stir-fry	174
Roast butternut squash risotto Ⓥ	176
Mixed mushroom and blue cheese gratin Ⓥ	180
Roast partridge with creamy polenta	182
Garlic-crusted racks of lamb	184
Autumn side dishes that go with everything Ⓥ	186

Puddings & bakes

Baked figs with honey and crème fraîche	188
Really easy apple and walnut muffins	190
Frosted pecan cake	192
Traditional toffee apples	194
Best-ever Bonfire Night cake	196
Cinnamon buns	198
Hot chocolate with a spicy twist	200
Savoury apple jelly	204
Luxury goes-with-everything chutney	206

IDEAL MENU SUGGESTION

Roast pumpkin soup with cheese straws
An Australian or Californian barrel-fermented Chardonnay is just the thing here

Chicken and sausage cassoulet
A Chianti Classico (red) or a Condrieu from the northern Rhône (white) are both great with cassoulet

Toffee apples

TRUSTED FOR ideal HOME SHOW OVER 100 YEARS

Roast pumpkin soup with dead-easy cheese straws

This rich-flavoured autumnal soup is fragrant with the soft spiciness of coriander, cumin and ginger, then topped with crunchy pumpkin seeds and a dash of sour crème fraîche. It's a blinder of a soup, and makes a good starter for a dinner, or a hearty lunch on its own.

prep 40 mins **cook** 1 hour–1 hour 10 mins SERVES 6-8

ingredients

2kg pumpkin or butternut squash
4 tbsp olive oil
Salt and freshly ground black pepper
2 garlic cloves, roughly chopped
1 onion, roughly chopped
1 tsp ground coriander
1 tsp ground cumin
½ tsp chilli flakes
2.5cm piece fresh root ginger, chopped
1 litre hot vegetable stock

For the cheese straws
500g packet puff pastry
A little plain flour
50g each Parmesan and Gruyère, grated

To serve
4 tbsp crème fraîche
1-2 tbsp toasted pumpkin seeds
Thyme sprigs

1 Preheat the oven to 200°C/180°C fan oven/gas mark 6. Peel the pumpkin or squash, remove the seeds and chop roughly. Put in a roasting tin, drizzle with 2 tbsp of the oil and season well. Roast in the oven for 20 minutes.

2 Add the garlic, onion, spices, ginger and remaining 2 tbsp oil, and mix together. Continue to roast for another 20-25 minutes until everything is tender. Set aside to cool a little.

3 Roll the pastry out on a clean, lightly floured surface until you have a large rectangle and sprinkle with the cheese. Fold each side in like a book, then roll out again to press the cheese into the pastry. Cut into 1cm strips and twist them like barley sugar. Chill for 10 minutes. Bake on a baking sheet for 10-15 minutes until golden. Cool on a wire rack.

4 Finish making the soup. Whiz the vegetables and stock together, in batches, until smooth. Return the soup to the pan, reheat gently and taste for seasoning.

5 Ladle among the bowls and top with crème fraîche, pumpkin seeds and thyme. Serve with the cheese straws.

"After blending, transfer to a sealable freezer-proof container, allow to cool and freeze for up to three months. When you're ready to eat it, thaw overnight at a cool temperature, then reheat."

Surprise vegetable parcels

The paper-thin filo pastry that wraps around these tasty pesto and vegetable parcels is the easiest thing to work with. Even better, there's no rolling or chilling required — just use it straight out of the packet. Visiting veggies will love these savoury treats, but so will everyone else, so make enough for the whole table.

prep 20 mins **cook** 20 mins SERVES 4

ingredients

4 tbsp olive oil
1 small aubergine, diced
1 each red and yellow pepper, deseeded and sliced
1 medium courgette, diced
1 garlic clove, sliced
Salt and freshly ground black pepper
275g filo pastry sheets

For the sauce
15g basil
10g Parmesan, grated
1 tbsp pine nuts, toasted, plus extra to sprinkle
Around 75ml olive oil

1 Heat 2 tbsp of the oil in a pan and fry the aubergine and peppers for 5 minutes over a medium heat, stirring every now and then until starting to turn golden. Add the courgette and garlic and continue frying for another 5 minutes, making sure the garlic doesn't burn. Set aside to cool a little. Preheat the oven to 200°C/180°C fan oven/gas mark 6. Put a baking sheet in the oven to preheat.

2 To make the pesto sauce, whiz the basil, Parmesan and pine nuts with the olive oil in a food processor. Season well.

3 Using 3 square sheets of pastry for each parcel, brush each sheet with a little of the remaining olive oil. Lay on top of each other at an angle so the points form a star. Place a quarter of the filling in the centre, drizzle with a little pesto and scatter over a few pine nuts, then gather up all the edges, pinching tightly to seal. Repeat to make four parcels. Brush with oil.

4 Place on the preheated baking tray. Bake for 15-20 minutes until golden and crisp. Serve with a mixed salad or vegetables.

"Depending on the brand of filo pastry, you may need to halve each sheet to make it square. Filo pastry dries out quickly, so keep the roll of unused sheets covered in a clean, damp J-cloth."

Posh coleslaw with Parma ham

Remoulade is a French classic involving chopped raw ingredients, mayonnaise and mustard. Celery's knobbly first cousin, celeriac is a winter vegetable with an earthy root flavour. You can either cook it, or serve it like this — raw with a punchy dressing and cured ham.

prep 20 mins SERVES 6

ingredients

150ml mayonnaise
1 tsp Dijon mustard
1 tbsp capers, drained and
　finely chopped
1 gherkin, finely chopped
1 celeriac
Juice of 1 lemon
Salt and freshly ground black
　pepper
Freshly chopped flat-leaf
　parsley, plus extra to
　garnish
12 slices cured ham, such as
　Parma or serrano

1 Put the mayonnaise, Dijon mustard, capers and gherkin in a bowl and stir together.

2 Peel the celeriac, cut into chunks and place in a bowl with the lemon juice to stop it from browning. Cut each piece into very thin strips (chefs call them 'juliennes') and return to the bowl.

3 Add the celeriac to the bowl with the mayonnaise mixture and season well. Sprinkle a little chopped parsley over, and mix everything together.

4 Divide between each plate alongside the ham, and garnish with parsley. Serve with toast and lemon wedges.

Sweetcorn, coriander and cumin fritters with chilli jam

These crispy vegetarian fritters are fantastic with chilli and ginger sauce as a starter. The heat of the chilli softens when it's cooked – for less of a fiery hit use just one chilli, but if you want to go for the burn, chuck in the seeds, too.

prep 15 mins **cook** 30 mins approx. SERVES 4

ingredients

For the fritters
150g plain flour
1 tsp baking powder
1 tsp ground cumin
Salt and freshly ground black
    pepper
2 eggs, beaten
100-150ml milk
2 shallots, finely chopped
1 tbsp fresh chopped coriander,
    plus extra to garnish
165g can sweetcorn, drained well
25g butter
1-2 tbsp vegetable oil

For the chilli jam
1 tbsp vegetable oil
1 red onion, finely chopped
2 garlic cloves, crushed
2 red chillies, deseeded and
    finely chopped
1 tbsp grated fresh root ginger
Juice of 1 lime
Zest and juice of 1 orange
2 tbsp demerara sugar
1 tbsp cider vinegar
2 tbsp tomato purée or tomato
    ketchup

1 Make the chilli jam. Heat the oil in a small pan, add the onion and cook for 10 minutes or until softened. Stir in the garlic, chillies and ginger and cook for 2 minutes.

2 Stir in the lime juice, orange zest and juice, sugar, vinegar and tomato purée (or ketchup). Bring to the boil, reduce the heat and simmer for 7-8 minutes. Cool, then spoon into a sterilised jar with a lid, and chill.

3 Make the fritters. Sift the flour and baking powder into a bowl, stir in the cumin and seasoning, make a well in the centre, add the eggs, and beat in enough milk to make a smooth batter (you may not need all of it).

4 Stir in the shallots, coriander and sweetcorn.

5 Heat a little of the butter and oil in a large frying pan. As soon as the butter has melted, add spoonfuls of the batter, well spaced apart around the pan and cook for 3-4 minutes. Flip over and continue to cook for a further 3 minutes until well risen and golden brown on both sides. Set aside on a plate. Carry on cooking the fritters until you've used up all the mixture, adding more butter and oil as necessary. Serve immediately with the chilli jam and garnished with coriander.

Pork crackling with apple sauce

Forget pork scratchings – this is the real deal. All you need is a piece of pork belly rind and a sharp scalpel to make the most unforgettably crisp and crunchy strips of porcine deliciousness. A side order of fluffy apple sauce is essential to cut through the richness.

prep 5 mins   cook 40-50 mins   SERVES 4

ingredients

500g piece pork rind
Sea salt
1 large cooking apple
2 cloves
Lemon zest
A little caster sugar

1 Preheat the oven to 220°C/200°C fan oven/gas mark 7.

2 Put the pork rind on a board and, armed with a scalpel fitted with a brand new blade, score the skin in neat thin slices. It is important to cut right through the rind so that as much fat as possible can cook out to give a really crunchy result.

3 Rub the rind side with salt and place in a roasting tin. Roast for 30 minutes. Take the tin out of the oven then carefully drain off the fat. The rind will be golden at this stage, but will probably have just crisped up round the edges, and will still be looking a bit flabby in the middle. Cut it into two or three smaller pieces and return to the tin and continue to cook, checking every 10 minutes or so until it's really crisp all over.

4 Meanwhile peel, core and chop the apple and place in a small pan with 2-3 tbsp water, the cloves and lemon zest. Cook gently until the apple falls to pieces and is tender. Add a little sugar to taste and more water, and then continue cooking to make a fluffy purée.

5 Break the crackling up into thin strips, spoon the apple sauce into a bowl, and serve immediately.

"Spoon the apple sauce into a warm bowl. Pile the pork strips onto a board, sprinkle liberally with salt again, plonk it in the middle of the table and let everyone dig in."

1) Michelin-starred chef **Jean-Christophe Novelli**, has an academy in Hertfordshire where he runs cookery courses. 2) Award-winning **Richard Phillips** has a clutch of thriving restaurants in Kent and is a regular on TV. 3) **Ed Baines** is chef and co-owner of London's Randall & Aubin. 4) **Susy Atkins** is a well-known wine writer.

3

4

AUTUMN MAINS ▶

Easy cod fish cakes with rocket sauce

Great fish cakes have a crisp crust and soft, melt-in-the-mouth filling. Make them a day ahead and chill them overnight in the fridge, then just put them in the oven for about 15 minutes once fried to ensure they're hot right through.

prep 45 mins, including 20 mins chilling **cook** 10 mins SERVES 4

ingredients

350g cod or haddock, cooked, skinned and boned
2 tbsp chopped fresh parsley
1 spring onion, finely chopped
Zest and juice of ½ lemon
Salt and freshly ground black pepper
350g creamy mashed potato
1 egg
75g fine white breadcrumbs
Plain flour
75g butter
1-2 tbsp oil

For the rocket sauce
Around 75ml olive oil
70g bag rocket
10g Parmesan or pecorino cheese, grated
A few drops of anchovy essence or a squeeze of lemon juice

1 Flake the fish into a bowl, then stir in the parsley, spring onion, lemon zest and juice, and season to taste.

2 Gently work in the potato to combine all the ingredients. Divide the mixture into eight rough portions, then shape each one into a fish cake. Put on a plate and chill well for 20 minutes.

3 For the rocket sauce, put the olive oil, rocket, cheese and anchovy essence or lemon juice in a food processor. Season well and blend until smooth. Set aside.

4 Beat the egg in a shallow bowl with 1 tbsp cold water and put the breadcrumbs in another. Sift 2 tbsp plain flour into a separate bowl. Dip the cakes in flour first, then egg, then breadcrumbs, so that they get an even coating. Repeat if you want a really thick crust.

5 Preheat the oven to 140°C/120°C fan oven/gas mark 1. Heat half the butter and oil in a frying pan and fry four fish cakes at a time for about 5 minutes, turning occasionally, until golden and crisp. Transfer to a plate and keep warm in the oven while the remaining fish cakes are being cooked.

6 Serve hot with the rocket sauce and salad.

"If you've any rocket sauce left over, serve it with pasta and a handful of chopped toasted walnuts for a quick supper."

Roast loin of pork

A great roast is satisfying, easy to cook and foolproof. Pork can be roasted as simply as you like – with sage, salt and pepper, say, or with a really straightforward stuffing like this one. Easy, no-fuss food.

prep 30 mins **cook** 2½ hours **SERVES** 6

ingredients

1 large loin of pork, around
    1.7kg, boned and rolled
A knob of butter
1 tsp olive oil
1 small red onion, finely
    chopped
40g fresh white breadcrumbs
1 tbsp chopped mixed sage and
    parsley
1 small dessert apple, peeled,
    cored and grated
3 dried apricots, finely chopped
A good grating of nutmeg
Salt and freshly ground black
    pepper
1 egg, beaten

For the gravy
1 tbsp plain flour
100ml dry white wine
450ml boiling water, light stock
    or water from the vegetables

1 Preheat the oven to 220°C/200°C fan oven/gas mark 7. Place the pork on a board.

2 Heat the butter and oil in a small pan until the butter has melted. Add the onion and cook for about 10-15 minutes over a low heat until softened.

3 Tip the softened onion into a bowl, cool a little and stir in the breadcrumbs, herbs, apple, apricots and nutmeg and season well. Add enough egg to bind the mixture together.

4 Have ready several pieces of string, cut in 30cm lengths. Unwrap the pork, skin-side down, on a board and season well. Spoon the stuffing into the pocket that naturally falls open when the meat is unwrapped. Starting from one long side, roll up and tie evenly at 2.5cm intervals. Make sure all the ties are on the underside. Place the pork in a roasting dish, rind upwards, with salt rubbed all over it.

5 Roast for 30 minutes, turning the tin round once. Then reduce the heat to 180°C/160°C fan oven/gas mark 4. Pour 300ml cold water into the bottom of the tin and continue to cook, allowing 30 minutes per 500g. Turn the tin round in the oven once again, and when cooked through, turn the heat off. Put the pork on a platter in the oven with the door slightly ajar. Allow to rest for at least 15 minutes while you make the gravy.

6 Drain all but 1 tbsp fat from the roasting tin. Put the tin on the hob, add the flour and cook over a medium heat for 1-2 minutes to make a paste. Add the wine, stirring all the time to dissolve the flour and any sticky meat juices in the tin. Allow to bubble for 2 minutes to cook off the alcohol. Gradually stir in the boiling water, stock or vegetable juices. Bring to a simmer and cook for 4-5 minutes to make a gravy. Season well. Serve with apple sauce (see page 156).

Corn on the cob with lime and coriander butter

Sun-ripened corn on the cob is a crowd-pleaser whether cooked over coals or simmered until the kernels turn bright yellow. Enjoy them slathered with butter mixed with chilli, herbs and spices.

prep 10 mins, plus chilling **cook** 10 mins SERVES 6

ingredients

175g salted butter, at room temperature
Zest and juice of 1 lime
Handful of fresh coriander leaves, chopped
1 red chilli, deseeded and chopped
1 garlic clove, crushed
1 tsp ground coriander
A dash or two of Tabasco
Salt and freshly ground black pepper
6 corn on the cob with skins

1 Light the barbecue and leave the coals to burn down until they're covered in a white ash. If you can still see flames, then it's not hot enough.

2 To make the flavoured butter, put the butter in a bowl and add the lime zest, juice, fresh coriander, chilli, garlic, ground coriander and Tabasco. Season well. Mix everything together, and spoon it onto a piece of greaseproof paper. Wrap it up and roll it to make into a rough sausage shape. Chill.

3 Pull off the outer leaves, and lay the cobs on the barbecue. Cook until golden, turning every now and then.

4 Add a knob of butter to the top of each cob, and serve with the remaining butter.

"If you want to boil the corn, resist adding salt to the water or the kernels may toughen. Instead, season the butter mixture well. Serve while they're still hot, otherwise the kernels will shrivel."

Chicken and sausage cassoulet

Originally regarded as peasant food, this nourishing French classic is named after the 'cassole', the earthenware pot in which it's cooked. Apparently it was traditional to use the browned, caramelised residue left in the pot from the previous cassoulet as a base for the next one. Stories abound of a single original cassoulet being extended this way for years!

prep 20 mins **cook** 30 mins SERVES 4

ingredients

1 tbsp sunflower oil
1 onion, roughly chopped
2 carrots, finely chopped
4-6 rashers streaky bacon, chopped
1 garlic clove, crushed
200g chicken breast, chopped
4 pork sausages, twisted in half
400g can of cannellini beans, drained
300ml hot chicken or vegetable stock
2 large tomatoes, chopped
1 tbsp lemon juice
2 tbsp freshly chopped mixed herbs, such as rosemary, sage or thyme
½ tsp each ground coriander and mixed spice
75g fresh white breadcrumbs
Salt and freshly ground black pepper
Butter

1 Heat the oil in a pan and cook the onion, carrots and bacon gently for about 10 minutes until starting to turn golden and all the fat has run out of the bacon. Stir in the garlic and cook for 1 minute.

2 Add the chicken and sausages and sauté until golden. Stir in the beans, stock, tomatoes, lemon juice and half the herbs. Mix gently. Give everything a really good stir and bring up to a simmer.

3 Preheat the oven to 200°C/180°C fan oven/gas mark 6. Transfer the chicken and sausage mixture to four individual ovenproof casserole pans. Mix together the spices, breadcrumbs, remaining herbs and season to taste. Spoon evenly over the meat and vegetable mixture to give a good coating and dot generously with butter.

4 Cook for 20-30 minutes or until crispy and slightly golden on top. Serve either with a crisp green salad, a tomato salad, or fresh green vegetables.

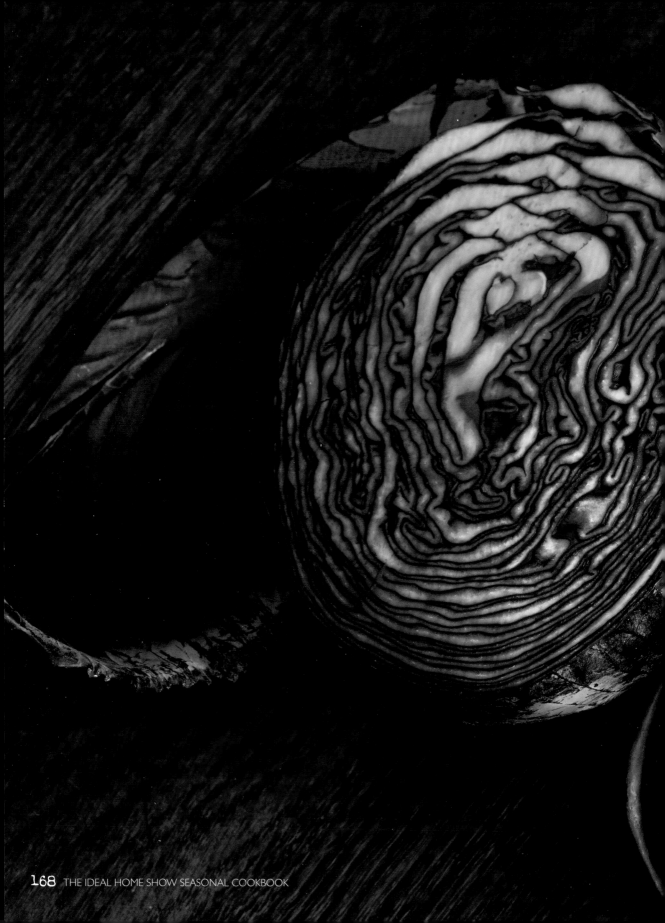

TOP TIP

Red cabbage has the longest lifespan of the entire vegetable family - it will literally keep for months in the fridge. What's more, it can be prepared any way you like: stir-fry it, braise it, steam it, or eat it raw in coleslaw.

MORE AUTUMN MAINS ▶

Polenta with pesto and charred mixed peppers

Polenta, made from cornmeal, has become fashionable in recent years alongside a great many so-called 'peasant' staples. Once cooked, it's usually left to firm up, then it's cut into pieces and served chargrilled, fried or toasted, with a sauce or vegetables.

prep 20 mins **cook** 40 mins SERVES 4 as a main course or 6 as a starter

ingredients

1 tsp salt
150g instant polenta
50g freshly grated Parmesan,
    plus extra for shaving
Salt and freshly ground black
    pepper
4 mixed peppers
1 red onion
6 tbsp olive oil
1 tsp balsamic vinegar
Vegetable or sunflower oil
2 tbsp pesto (see recipe on
    page 150)
Fresh basil leaves and toasted
    pine nuts, to garnish

1 Bring 1 litre water to the boil in a large pan, add the salt then gradually pour in the polenta, stirring. Whisk until smooth and then reduce the heat to a gentle simmer. Cook for about 5 minutes, stirring frequently with a wooden spoon until thickened. Polenta is quite dry, so check frequently that it's not catching and burning on the bottom of the pan.

2 Immediately beat in the cheese and seasoning, and transfer the mixture to a rectangular tin (about 19 × 28cm) lined with baking parchment, flatten the top and leave for around 20 minutes until set firm.

3 Halve and deseed the peppers and cut them into large cubes. Peel the onion and cut into wedges, making sure the root is holding each piece so that it keeps its shape. Heat about 2 tbsp of the olive oil in a pan and cook the peppers and onion briskly until beginning to colour. Stir in the remaining olive oil and vinegar, and season to taste. Set aside until ready to serve.

4 Turn the polenta out onto a large clean board and cut into slices or triangles. Brush well with vegetable oil. Heat 1-2 tbsp of vegetable or sunflower oil in a griddle pan and fry the polenta for 3-4 minutes on each side until golden and nicely ridge-marked.

5 Serve slices of polenta topped with the peppers and onion, drizzle the pesto over, and garnish with basil and pine nuts, plus shavings of Parmesan. Great either hot, warm or chilled.

Can't-go-wrong carrot and parsnip rösti

Although usually made with potato, these Swiss vegetable cakes are just as good when you use other vegetables — sweet carrots and earthy parsnips, for example. They're also a terrific side dish served with slices of roast meat, or a dollop of hummus for vegetarians.

prep 20 mins **cook** 6-7 mins SERVES 4

ingredients

1 spring onion, finely chopped
2 garlic cloves, crushed
225g each carrots and parsnips
1 tbsp each chopped chives and parsley
Salt and freshly ground black pepper
Freshly grated nutmeg
Zest and juice of ½ lemon
1 medium egg, beaten
Plain flour
Sunflower oil and butter, for frying

1 Preheat the oven to 170°C/150°C fan oven/gas mark 3. In a large bowl mix the spring onion and garlic; then, using a coarse grater, grate the carrots and parsnips into it. Stir in most of the herbs, season with the salt, pepper and nutmeg, and add the lemon zest and juice.

2 Stir in enough egg to bind the mixture without making it too wet. Shape into eight flat, round patties, then dust with flour.

3 Heat a little oil and butter in a frying pan and fry three or four at a time for 2-3 minutes each side until crisp and golden. Drain on kitchen paper and keep hot in the oven while you cook the rest.

"To serve this as a starter, divide two rösti between four plates, top them with a spoonful of soured cream and a slice of Parma ham, and serve with a wedge of lemon to squeeze over."

Beef and citrus stir-fry

A good piece of steak that's sliced and stir-fried will go a long way, but it needs a bit of embellishment: add a touch of zingy citrus fruit and green chilli to make this a really easy and quick stir-fry supper.

prep 15 mins **cook** 7-8 mins SERVES 4

ingredients

500g sirloin or rump steak,
  trimmed
Juice of 1 grapefruit
1 green chilli, finely chopped
2-3 tbsp olive oil
300g egg noodles
2 onions, sliced
1 red pepper, deseeded and
  diced
200g sprouting broccoli, stems
  halved
3-4 tbsp stock
2 tsp cornflour
2 tbsp dry sherry
2 satsumas, peeled and
  segmented
Salt

1 Cut the beef into strips. Mix the grapefruit juice, green chilli and 1 tbsp oil in a shallow dish, then add the beef and mix lightly. Set aside. Cook the noodles, according to the packet instructions, and drain well.

2 In a wok or large frying pan, heat a little oil and fry the onions until softened. Drain the meat (reserving the marinade) and fry quickly with the onions, then add the pepper and sprouting broccoli, and cook for only 2-3 minutes.

3 Mix together the reserved marinade, stock, cornflour and sherry and stir into the meat along with the satsuma segments.

4 Stir-fry for another 1-2 minutes until the sauce thickens. Add salt to taste and serve with the egg noodles.

"Takeaway boxes like the one in the photo are readily available online, and ideal for a fireworks party."

Roast butternut squash risotto

A whole squash hollowed out and roasted until tender makes for an eye-catching and edible serving dish for this vegetarian risotto.

prep 10 mins **cook** 40 mins **SERVES 4**

ingredients

- 4 small squash, such as acorn and harlequin
- 3 tbsp olive oil, plus extra for roasting
- Salt and freshly ground black pepper
- A few sprigs of fresh thyme
- 1 small butternut squash, peeled and chopped into 1cm pieces
- 1 small glass white wine or stock
- 1 litre hot vegetable stock
- 6 shallots, finely chopped
- 50g butter
- 300g risotto rice
- 2 tsp finely chopped sage
- 3 tbsp grated Parmesan cheese

1 Preheat the oven to 200°C/180°C fan oven/gas mark 6. Cut the top off each of the small squash using a sharp knife. Scoop out the seeds and rub a little oil inside each and season well.

2 Put the prepared small squash on a baking tray, then sprinkle with some thyme leaves. Roast in the oven for 30-40 minutes or until softened and browning. Meanwhile, cook the chopped butternut squash, seasoned well and with a drizzle of olive oil, in a roasting tray underneath the small squash for about 20 minutes until golden and tender. Make sure they don't burn.

3 While all the squash is cooking, gently heat the wine or stock in a pan. In a separate casserole pan, fry the shallots in the oil and 25g of the butter until softened, then add the rice and the sage. Stir for a few minutes until well coated with oil, then gradually add the vegetable stock mixture, a ladleful at a time.

4 Keep stirring and, as each ladleful is absorbed, pour in more liquid until the rice is tender but still has a slight bite. Add the remaining butter, sage, cheese and chopped squash, and check the seasoning. Remove from the heat, cover and leave to sit for 2-3 minutes.

5 Put a whole squash on each plate and spoon the risotto inside. Garnish with sage leaves (see tip below) and serve.

"Garnish with fried sage leaves. Heat a knob of butter and a drizzle of oil in a pan. Drop in 4-8 small sage leaves and fry until crisp. Drain on kitchen paper and season."

TOP TIP
Chopped fennel is a good
substitute for celery in a
tomato pasta sauce, giving it
a subtle hint of aniseed.

TRUSTED FOR
· ideal ·
HOME SHOW
OVER 100 YEARS

MORE AUTUMN MAINS ▶

Mixed mushroom and blue cheese gratin

This is a really rich main course for a special dinner that's as popular with dyed-in-the-wool vegetarians as it is with carnivores. It's warm and comforting, and best wolfed down with crusty bread and a crisp green salad.

prep 30 mins **cook** 30 mins SERVES 4

ingredients

750g potatoes
25g butter
2 small garlic cloves, crushed
675g mushrooms, such as oyster, shiitake, field, button, brown, wiped and cut into even-sized pieces
1-2 tbsp cornflour
100ml vegetable stock or red wine
2 tbsp chopped fresh mixed herbs
200g Roquefort cheese, crumbled
3-4 tbsp thick cream or Greek yoghurt
Salt and freshly ground black pepper
Butter, melted

1 Put the potatoes in a pan and bring to the boil. Simmer for 5-8 minutes until parboiled. Drain well, and slice into rounds.

2 Melt the butter in a large pan, add the garlic and mushrooms and cook gently for 3-4 minutes or until the mushrooms are just softened. Remove with a slotted spoon and set aside.

3 Mix the cornflour with a little stock to form a paste, and then add to the pan and cook gently, stirring all the time, until thickened, adding more stock until you have a smooth sauce. Add the herbs, cheese and cream, stir gently until blended, and then add seasoning to taste.

4 Preheat the oven to 200°C/180°C fan oven/gas mark 6. Stir the mushrooms into the wine and cheese sauce, and transfer to four individual dishes. Top with the sliced potatoes and drizzle over the melted butter. Bake for 15-20 minutes until the potatoes are tender, golden and crispy.

"For an alternative topping to potatoes, finish off each dish with scrunched-up filo pastry, drizzle with melted butter and bake until crisp and golden."

Roast partridge with creamy polenta

August 12 – better known as 'The Glorious 12th' – heralds the start of the game season, when the first grouse appear on plates around the nation. But it isn't until September 1 that partridge can be roasted for the table. This deep-flavoured meat provides delicious juices for making gravy, so it needs little more than soft, spoonable polenta and tender, buttered Chantenay carrots.

prep 15 mins **cook** 25 mins SERVES 4

ingredients

4 prepared, ready-to-roast
  partridge
A little butter, softened
Salt and freshly ground black
  pepper
6-8 rashers streaky bacon
2 shallots, thinly sliced
2-3 garlic cloves, sliced
Thyme sprigs
125ml red wine
125ml hot chicken stock
2 tsp plain flour
100g instant polenta
100ml single cream or milk
Parmesan cheese, grated

1 Preheat the oven to 190°C/170°C fan oven/gas mark 5. Wipe the birds dry inside and out. Rub with butter and sprinkle with seasoning inside and out. Lay two strips of bacon evenly over each partridge and tie with string.

2 Arrange the shallots and garlic in the base of a snug-fitting, flameproof roasting tin, along with a few sprigs of thyme. Place the birds on top and pour around a small glass of water and half the wine and stock.

3 Roast for 15 minutes, then turn them all round so the inside edge of each partridge faces out. Return to the oven for a further 5-10 minutes or until golden and the juices run clear. For larger birds, they may need 10 minutes or so longer.

4 Transfer the birds to a warm serving plate, cover with foil and leave in a warm place to rest.

5 Put the roasting tin on the hob and whisk in the flour. Cook for 1 minute until thick and bubbling. Add the rest of the wine and stock and bring gently to the boil, stirring well. Bubble until slightly thickened, then season to taste.

6 Boil 300ml water in a pan, tip in the polenta and whisk quickly, breaking up any lumps. Cook for 1 minute for soft polenta, then stir in the cream, Parmesan and a little seasoning. Keep stirring until well blended and ready to serve.

7 Serve a spoonful of polenta with the partridges, and pour the sauce over.

"Polenta thickens up very quickly, so serve it as soon as it's ready, or add extra milk to maintain the soft consistency of mashed potato."

Garlic-crusted racks of lamb

Best-end rack of lamb is easy to cook, easy to carve and gives you two to three individual portions of super-tender cutlets. When trimmed the French way, you're left with small, clean bones for easy finger-eating and two to three bites of succulent, juicy meat.

prep 20 mins (if ready-trimmed) **cook** 20-45 mins **SERVES 4-6**

ingredients

2 good-sized racks of lamb,
    with 6-7 cutlets per rack
3 tbsp breadcrumbs
3 tbsp finely chopped mixed
    herbs, such as parsley,
    marjoram, rosemary and
    thyme
2 garlic cloves, crushed
Finely grated zest of 1 lemon
A good squeeze of lemon juice
Salt and freshly ground black
    pepper
25g butter

1 Preheat the oven to 220°C/200°C fan oven/gas mark 7. Put the racks on a board.

2 Mix the breadcrumbs, herbs, garlic, lemon zest and juice together and season well. Spread the butter over the outside of the lamb then press the breadcrumb and herb mixture evenly over the top to coat them well. Leave for 30 minutes at room temperature before roasting.

3 Place the racks upright in a small roasting tin and cook for 15 minutes for pink, 20-25 minutes for medium and 30-35 minutes for well cooked. However, the cooking time may be a little longer, depending on the thickness of the rack. Check by feeling the lamb: if it's still very fleshy, continue to cook for a few minutes longer. Cover and leave to rest for 4-5 minutes before carving.

"A pile of creamy mash and tender sprigs of purple sprouting broccoli are the perfect side order. Pile the mash into a fluffy mound in the middle of the plate and scatter the broccoli around. Carve the racks, then position on top of the potato, allowing two to three cutlets per person. Drizzle any rested juices from the tin around the plate."

Autumn side dishes that go with everything

Boiled, steamed, sautéed or stir-fried, these simple vegetable side dishes will add a punch to roasts, pan-fried fish, meat, griddled cheese or a terrific tart.

V Mushrooms with shallots and thyme

Heat 1 tbsp oil and 15g butter in a pan and sauté 3 chopped shallots until golden. Add 250g chestnut mushrooms, halved or quartered, season well, and stir-fry until the mushrooms start to colour. Add 1 tbsp sherry vinegar, a few sprigs of thyme and season well. Cook until the vinegar reduces and evaporates. Serve.

V Stir-fried red cabbage with red onions and pine nuts

Put 25g sultanas in a bowl and cover with boiling water. Heat 1 tbsp oil in a pan and sauté 1 finely sliced red onion until starting to soften. Add ½ finely sliced red cabbage and continue to cook, stir-frying and tossing the cabbage in the pan every now and then for about 5 minutes until the cabbage is cooked but still has a slight bite to it. Drain the sultanas and add to the pan with 25g pine nuts. Season well, add a squeeze of orange juice and knob of butter and sprinkle with parsley. Toss everything together again and serve.

 Roasted beetroot with feta and spinach

Peel (using rubber gloves if you don't want pink fingertips) 6-8 whole beetroot, quarter and put in a roasting tin. Drizzle with 1-2 tbsp oil and roast in the oven at 200°C/180°C fan oven/gas mark 6 for 30-40 minutes until tender. After 20 minutes, cut 1 red onion into wedges and add to the tin and drizzle with oil, with a couple of sprigs of chopped rosemary. Continue to roast. Spoon the beetroot mixture into a bowl. Add 100g feta cheese, broken into pieces, and a few handfuls of spinach. Drizzle with balsamic vinegar, season well and serve.

 Root vegetable mash with herb butter

Peel 750g floury potatoes, ½ celeriac, and 1 large parsnip. Roughly chop. Put the potatoes in a pan of cold salted water. Cover, bring to the boil and simmer for 10 minutes. Add the celeriac and parsnip and continue to boil for a further 10 minutes until tender. Beat together 40g softened butter and 3 tbsp freshly chopped herbs. Drain the vegetables well and return to the pan. Place over the heat and cook for a minute or two to drive off any moisture. Add a good splash of milk, season well, and mash with half the butter. Spoon into a bowl and top with remaining herb butter.

Baked figs with honey and crème fraîche

Purple or green figs, fat and full of fragrance, are a mouth-watering sight in late summer on trees all over Europe. Baking them with a drizzle of honey brings out their sweetness and needs no more than crème fraîche and fresh orange zest to cut through the richness.

prep 5 mins **cook** 10 mins **SERVES 4**

ingredients

8 fresh green or purple figs
4 tbsp acacia honey
4 tbsp crème fraîche
1 tsp finely grated orange zest

1 Preheat the oven to 180°C/160°C fan oven/gas mark 4. Wipe the figs and cut them into quarters, but not all the way through. Squeeze each base gently so it opens like a flower.

2 Place the figs in a small ovenproof dish and drizzle with half the honey. Bake for 10 minutes just to warm through.

3 To serve, top each one with a swirl of crème fraîche, sprinkle with the orange zest, then drizzle over the remaining honey.

"Serve them with pistachio and almond biscuits:
Preheat the oven to 200°C/180°C fan oven/gas mark 6. Beat together 50g softened butter and 40g icing sugar in a bowl until soft and creamy. Sift 75g plain flour and 25g ground almonds into the bowl. Sprinkle 15g finely chopped pistachio nuts on top. Knead well to bring the ingredients together to make a dough. Shape into 12 balls and place on a large baking sheet lined with parchment. Use a fork to mark the top of each, pressing down slightly to flatten. Bake for 10-12 minutes until just golden round the edges. Cool and dust with icing sugar, then serve with the figs. Heavenly."

Really easy apple and walnut muffins

Muffins require no special kitchen skills – anyone can make them. The only trick is avoiding over-mixing the batter. Light strokes for about 10 seconds will do it – any more than that and you'll get dry, tough offerings.

prep 15 mins **cook** 30 mins MAKES 12

ingredients

350g plain flour
½ tsp salt
2 tsp ground cinnamon
3 tsp baking powder
75g golden caster sugar
2 crisp sweet apples, about 225g, cored and diced
100g sultanas
50g walnuts, roughly chopped, plus a few extra for the topping
2 eggs, beaten
175ml milk
100g butter, melted and cooled
Demerara sugar, to sprinkle

1 Preheat the oven to 190°C/170°C fan oven/gas mark 5. Line a 12-hole muffin tin with paper cases.

2 Sift the flour, salt, cinnamon and baking powder into a bowl and add the sugar. Add the chopped apple, sultanas and walnuts and toss all the ingredients together to roughly mix them up.

3 Beat the eggs, milk and melted butter together in a separate bowl or jug, then stir into the dry ingredients. Now, don't over-mix the batter – just combine the wet and the dry ingredients briefly and roughly – it's fine if there are still a few floury patches.

4 Spoon the mixture evenly into the muffin cases. Chop the extra walnuts and sprinkle over the top with a little demerara sugar. Bake for 30 minutes or until well risen and just firm to the touch.

"Enjoy these as a pudding: serve them warm from the oven with a ball of vanilla ice cream melting over the top."

Frosted pecan cake

An impressively rich nut and chocolate sponge contrasts perfectly with snowy, lighter-than-air icing known as 'American frosting': it's made from icing sugar whisked together with egg whites over simmering water that cooks the whites – the closest thing to gorging on a cloud.

prep 40 mins cook 30 mins SERVES 10-12

ingredients

225g unsalted butter, plus extra to grease
175g pecan halves
350g golden caster sugar
5 medium eggs
350g plain flour
1½ tsp baking powder
½ tsp salt
2 tsp ground cinnamon
1 tsp ground nutmeg
1 tsp vanilla essence
2-3 tbsp milk

For the frosting and filling
350g icing sugar
3 large egg whites, at room temperature
4-6 tbsp chocolate and nut spread

1 Preheat the oven to 180°C/160°C fan oven/gas mark 4. Grease and line two 20cm sponge tins with greaseproof paper.

2 Set aside 10 pecan halves. Place the rest on a baking tray and roast for 10 minutes, then whiz briefly in a food processor until chopped. Don't over-process or they'll become greasy.

3 Cream the butter and sugar until pale and fluffy and then beat in the eggs, one at a time, adding around a tbsp of flour every now and then to prevent the mixture from separating. Sift over the remaining flour, baking powder, salt and spices and carefully fold in with the chopped nuts, vanilla and milk to give a fairly soft dropping consistency.

4 Divide evenly between the tins, then bake for around 30 minutes. Cool the cakes in the tin for 10 minutes, then turn out and transfer to a wire rack to cool completely.

5 For the frosting, sift the icing sugar into a large mixing bowl. Add the egg whites, then place the bowl over a pan of simmering water, making sure the base doesn't touch the water. Whisk with an electric whisk, gradually increasing the speed, until the mixture is thick, glossy and stands in peaks.

6 Cut each sponge through the middle to make two thin layers. Place one of the sponge bases on a board or serving plate and then layer up the sponges with a little of the frosting, using the chocolate spread only on the middle layer. Spread the sides and top with the rest of the white frosting. Roughly chop the remaining pecans and scatter over.

"Freeze pecan cake for up to three months wrapped in clingfilm. Thaw slowly by leaving it out overnight, then unwrap it and complete the recipe from Step 5."

Traditional toffee apples

A crust of rich toffee encasing a crisp, new-season apple is a wonderful way to celebrate autumn. If you can't get hold of wooden lollipop sticks, use wooden chopsticks split in two.

prep 10 mins cook 20 mins approx. SERVES 6

ingredients

6 dessert apples
Sunflower oil, for brushing
400g granulated sugar
175g golden syrup

1 Pull out any apple stems and push a wooden stick into the core. Line a baking sheet with baking parchment and brush lightly with oil.

2 Put the sugar, 250ml water and golden syrup into a heavy-based pan and stir over a moderate heat to dissolve the sugar.

3 Increase the heat and bring the mixture to the boil. Continue to boil without stirring until the temperature reaches 150°C on a sugar thermometer, or becomes hard enough to crack easily (see tip below).

4 The toffee will be boiling hot at this point. Carefully dip each apple into the mixture and twist around to coat all over. Sit each on the baking parchment and leave to set.

"Use a good-quality, heavy-based pan. Timings vary according to its shape: a wide, shallow pan with a larger surface area allows the mixture to reach the toffee stage more quickly."

"No sugar thermometer? Simmer the sugar mixture for around 15-20 minutes. As it cooks, the surface bubbles become smaller and the mixture darkens. Drop a teaspoonful of the sugar mixture into a glass of cold water - it's ready when it hardens enough for you to crack it. If it's still soft, continue to boil it for a few more minutes."

Autumn puddings & bakes

Best-ever Bonfire Night cake

Hands up anyone who knew that the traditional treat on Bonfire Night is a cake called 'Parkin'? Flavoured with the rich, dark taste of treacle and with a texture from heaven, it hails from the north of England…or maybe from Wales…or then again, maybe Scotland — there are as many variations as there are days in the week.

prep 20 mins **cook** 45-50 mins MAKES ABOUT 18 PIECES

ingredients

50g butter, plus a little extra for greasing
125g self-raising flour
100g porridge oats
50g oatmeal
125g light muscovado sugar
1 tsp ground ginger
125g black treacle
100ml milk
1 large egg

1 Preheat the oven to 170°C/150°C fan oven/gas mark 3. Grease and line a 23cm square tin with greaseproof paper.

2 Mix the flour, oats, oatmeal, sugar and ground ginger in a bowl. Put the treacle in a pan with the butter and milk and heat gently until the butter has just melted. Pour into the bowl with the dry ingredients and add the egg. Beat everything together well, and spoon into the tin.

3 Bake in the oven for 45-50 minutes. Cool in the tin for 30 minutes, then transfer to a rack to cool completely. Upturn onto a board and peel off the greaseproof paper. Turn the right way up and cut into fingers. Wrap well in clingfilm and store in an airtight container for up to five days, or freeze for up to three months.

Cinnamon buns

Finding potato in a list of ingredients for cinnamon buns may seem a bit weird, but yeast responds brilliantly to its starchy quality, which, in turn, gives a wonderfully light and fluffy texture. These are best eaten fresh, so make a big batch and freeze some, un-iced, for another time.

prep 30 mins **cook** 30 mins, plus resting and proving MAKES 12 BUNS

ingredients

For the bun dough

250g potatoes, peeled and cubed

3 tbsp granulated sugar

2 tbsp ready-to-use dry yeast

750g plain flour, plus extra to dust

½ tsp salt

75g butter, melted

2 eggs, beaten

For the filling

125g brown sugar

1 tbsp ground cinnamon

75g softened butter

For the icing

175g icing sugar

50ml water

"Ring the changes with a cream cheese icing: beat 125g full-fat cream cheese and 30g softened butter together in a bowl. Gradually add 175g icing sugar, beating well after each addition, then finally stir in 3 tbsp whipping cream."

1 Boil the potatoes in a pan of salted water for 15 minutes, or until tender. Drain, return to the pan, add all but ½ tsp sugar to the potatoes, and mash well. Leave to cool completely.

2 Meanwhile, in a large bowl dissolve the remaining sugar in 250ml warm water. Sprinkle the yeast into this mixture and set aside for about 10 minutes, or until frothy. Whisk to incorporate the yeast into the liquid.

3 Sift the flour and salt into a large bowl. Make a well in the centre and add the butter, cooled potato mixture, beaten eggs and yeast liquid. Use a round-bladed table knife to mix all the ingredients together, and then use your hands to knead the mixture. If it feels dry, add another drizzle of water. Continue to knead for about 5 minutes until smooth. You can also do this stage in a freestanding mixer using a dough hook. Place in a clean bowl, cover and leave to rise for about 40 minutes until doubled in volume.

4 To make the filling, mix the sugar and cinnamon together in a bowl. Take the dough out of the bowl and gently knead it on a board or clean work surface lightly dusted with flour. Roll it out until it measures around 35 x 50cm. Carefully spread the butter over the dough, then sprinkle with the sugar mixture. Starting at one long side, roll up tightly and pinch the seams to close them. Using a serrated knife, cut into 12 pieces and place in a parchment lined roasting tin. Cover and leave to rise for 30 minutes, or until doubled in size. Preheat the oven to 190°C/170°C fan oven/gas mark 5.

5 Uncover and bake for about 30 minutes or until well risen and golden. They're ready when they sound hollow when lightly tapped on the top. Lift out of the roasting tin and cool on a wire rack until just warm.

6 Mix together the icing sugar and water and drizzle over the buns, then serve immediately.

Hot chocolate with a spicy twist

Here's an indulgent way to round off supper instead of a pudding. It's super-quick to make and the dark chocolate gives the drink a silky richness. No need to add sugar – the chocolate provides plenty of sweetness.

prep 5 mins cook 10 mins SERVES 6-8

ingredients

1.5 litres milk
1½ tsp ground cinnamon
½ tsp ground cardamom
200g dark chocolate, minimum 70% cocoa solids, roughly chopped, plus extra for shaving
100ml extra-thick double cream

1 Pour the milk into a pan, sprinkle over the spices, and bring to a gentle boil.

2 Add the chocolate, turn down the heat and let the milk simmer gently, stirring every now and then until the chocolate has melted.

3 Divide among six or eight glasses. Lightly whip the cream, and spoon on top with some chocolate shavings. Enjoy immediately!

"For hot milk chocolate, use the same quantity of chocolate, but with 30-50% cocoa solids. Want to add a splash of booze? Brandy, whisky or a liqueur are ideal: pour it in with the milk, and before adding the chocolate, let it simmer for 1 minute to cook off some of the alcohol."

TOP TIP
A glut of cooking apples makes a brilliant compote.
Peel, chop and simmer in water with sugar, lemon
zest and sultanas until soft and fluffy.

Savoury apple jelly

This is a great autumn accompaniment to game, cold roast pork, ham, meat pies and cheese, and it stores well for Christmas. Go as hot as you dare with red chilli: try fiery bird's eye or fruity Scotch bonnet – the heat will be tempered by the sweetness, anyway. Don't peel and core the apples, as these contain the precious pectin that makes the jelly set. But be sure you remove all the bruised bits: if these end up in the pulp, they may stop the jelly from setting.

prep 45 mins, plus overnight (for the liquid to drip from the pulp)
cook 1 hour MAKES 2-3KG

ingredients

2kg firm cooking apples or a mixture of apples (all bruises and blemishes removed), roughy chopped
1.5 litres water
250ml cider vinegar
2 cloves
Granulated sugar
1-2 hot red chillies, deseeded and very finely chopped (2 for hot, 1 for mild)

1 Place the prepared fruit and water in a large pan or preserving pan and bring to the boil. Simmer gently for around 30 minutes until the fruit is very soft.

2 Prepare a jelly bag and stand. Place a large bowl underneath and ladle in the fruit mixture. Leave to drip overnight. Resist pressing the jelly bag, as this will make the finished jelly cloudy.

3 Discard pulp and measure liquid into a clean preserving pan. Add vinegar (noting volume) and cloves, and bring to the boil.

4 Add 450g sugar per 600ml liquid and stir to dissolve. Bring slowly up to the boil again. If you're using a preserving thermometer, put it in now. Chill two plates in the freezer.

5 Simmer over a steady medium heat until it reaches the setting point. If you're using a preserving thermometer, check the temperature – if you're not, it should take around 30-40 minutes. As soon as it reaches 105°C, turn down the heat so that the mercury doesn't go any higher – it needs to hold this temperature for about 5 minutes. To check that it's set, take the pan off the heat, put a spoonful of the hot liquid onto a chilled saucer, then return the saucer to the freezer for 30 seconds or so. Next, run your finger across the mixture – it's ready when it wrinkles.

6 When the setting point is reached, take the pan off the heat and discard the cloves. After a couple of minutes, carefully stir in the chillies. Leave to settle for about 10 minutes.

7 Have several sterilised heated jars ready (see page 304). Ladle the jelly into them and top with waxed discs and sterilised lids. Label and keep in a cool, dark place.

Luxury goes-with-everything chutney

A stonkingly good dark chutney that will happily sit next to a punchy Cheddar, liven up a slice of cold roast ham, or be spread over Middle Eastern hummus on a baguette. It's quick to make and improves with time, too.

prep 30 mins **cook** 2 hours MAKES ABOUT 1KG

ingredients

350g mixed dried fruits (use at least half of apricots, prunes, or figs for luxury, then top up with the cheaper dried fruits such as sultanas and raisins)

1 large onion, finely chopped

750g dark brown sugar

2 tsp curry powder

2 tsp allspice

2 tsp cinnamon

A good pinch of cayenne pepper

600ml liquid (use the fruit soaking liquid made up with red wine vinegar or sherry vinegar)

3 ripe Williams or Conference pears, cored and finely chopped

1 Cover the dried fruit with boiling water and soak for half an hour or so. Gently soften the finely chopped onion in a large pan with a little brown sugar and 100ml water for 10-15 minutes over a low heat.

2 Drain the dried fruit (saving the liquor) and whiz very briefly in a food processor with a couple of tablespoons of the liquor or vinegar – you only want to chop the fruit, not purée it. Place it in the pan with the onions and add all the other ingredients, except the pears.

3 Simmer uncovered for about 30 minutes, then add the prepared pears and continue for a further 45 minutes or so until the chutney has thickened. Pour into sterilised jars (see page 304), cover and label when cooled.

"Always store preserves in a cool, dark cupboard to mature. As soon as they are opened, they need to be kept in the fridge."

WINTER

BEST IN SEASON

WINTER

December

Apples (late and stored), Brussels sprouts, Brussels tops, cabbages (green, red and white), carrots, celeriac, celery, chestnuts, chicory, endive, Jerusalem artichokes, kale, leeks, lettuce, mushrooms, onions, parsnips, potatoes, rhubarb (forced), spring greens, swede, turnips, winter greens

Grouse (until 10 December), hare, mallard, partridge, pheasant, snipe, wild duck, woodcock, wood pigeon

Cod, crab, mussels, oysters (rock and native), sea bass, whiting

January

Apples (stored), Brussels sprouts, Brussels tops, cabbages (green, red and white), celery, chestnuts, chicory, endive, Jerusalem artichokes, kale, leeks, lettuce, mushrooms, onions, parsnips, pears (stored), potatoes, rhubarb (forced), spring greens, swede, winter greens

Hare, partridge, pheasant, snipe, wild duck, woodcock

Cockles, cod, crab, oysters, whiting

February

Apples (stored), Brussels sprouts, Brussels tops, cabbages (green and white), chicory, endive, Jerusalem artichokes, kale, leeks, lettuce, mushrooms, onions, potatoes, rhubarb (forced), spring greens, swede, winter greens

Hare, wild duck

Cockles, cod, crab, rock oysters

Winter

Starters

Mains

Puddings

IDEAL MENU SUGGESTION

TRUSTED FOR · ideal · HOME SHOW OVER 100 YEARS

super-quick salmon pâté
Try an Australian Chardonnay from Margaret River or Pouilly-Fumé from the Loire

No-fuss Christmas turkey and all the trimmings
A white Hermitage (Rhône) or a red Bordeaux (Graves) are spot on for traditional Christmas fare

Best-ever Christmas pudding

Duck, pork and chicken terrine with wild mushrooms

With its impressive layers of meat, mushrooms and dried fruit parcelled up in colourful strips of streaky bacon, this terrine is a sight to behold – a brilliant stand-by for feeding a crowd over Christmas. Serve it with punchy piccalilli, crusty bread, pickled onions and mouth-puckering sour cornichons (baby gherkins).

prep 40 mins **cook** 1 hour 20 mins **SERVES 12**

ingredients

1 tbsp sunflower or olive oil, plus extra for brushing
225g mixed mushrooms, sliced (use wild when in season)
25g dried cranberries or sour cherries
Truffle oil
Salt and ground white pepper
225g streaky bacon rashers
About 525g raw meat of wild duck, pheasant or partridge
About 325g pork fillet, trimmed
Pinch of mixed spice
1 large free-range egg, beaten
6 tbsp brandy or cognac
450g chicken breast, thinly sliced
Piccalilli, to serve

1 Preheat the oven to 200°C/180°C fan oven/gas mark 6. Heat 1 tbsp oil in a pan and fry the mushrooms until tender and the liquid evaporated. Stir in the cranberries, followed by a few drops of truffle oil and seasoning, and set aside to cool.

2 Put the bacon on a board and stretch each rasher using the back of a table knife. Brush a little oil around the inside of a 900g loaf tin, then lay each strip widthways along the tin to line it, and continue until the base and sides are completely covered. You'll have a couple of rashers left over to cover the top.

3 Finely mince the duck, pheasant or partridge and pork separately in a food processor. Put in a bowl with the mixed spice, egg and 2-3 tbsp brandy. Season well and combine everything thoroughly. Season the chicken and pour the rest of the brandy over.

4 Press half the minced mixture into the base, then the layer of chicken strips, and then the layer of mushrooms. Top with the remaining mixture and press down to flatten the top. Cover with remaining bacon. Cover with foil and place in a roasting tin. Fill the tin with warm water to half the depth of the terrine and place in the oven.

5 Bake for 60-80 minutes, depending on the depth of the tin. Remove the loaf tin from the roasting tin and place on a rack in a cool place (this allows the air to circulate underneath it to cool it more quickly). Once cool, put a light weight on top and press down gently and chill overnight.

6 Run a palette knife around the edge and upturn onto a board. Turn the right way up, slice and serve with piccalilli.

WINTER STARTERS

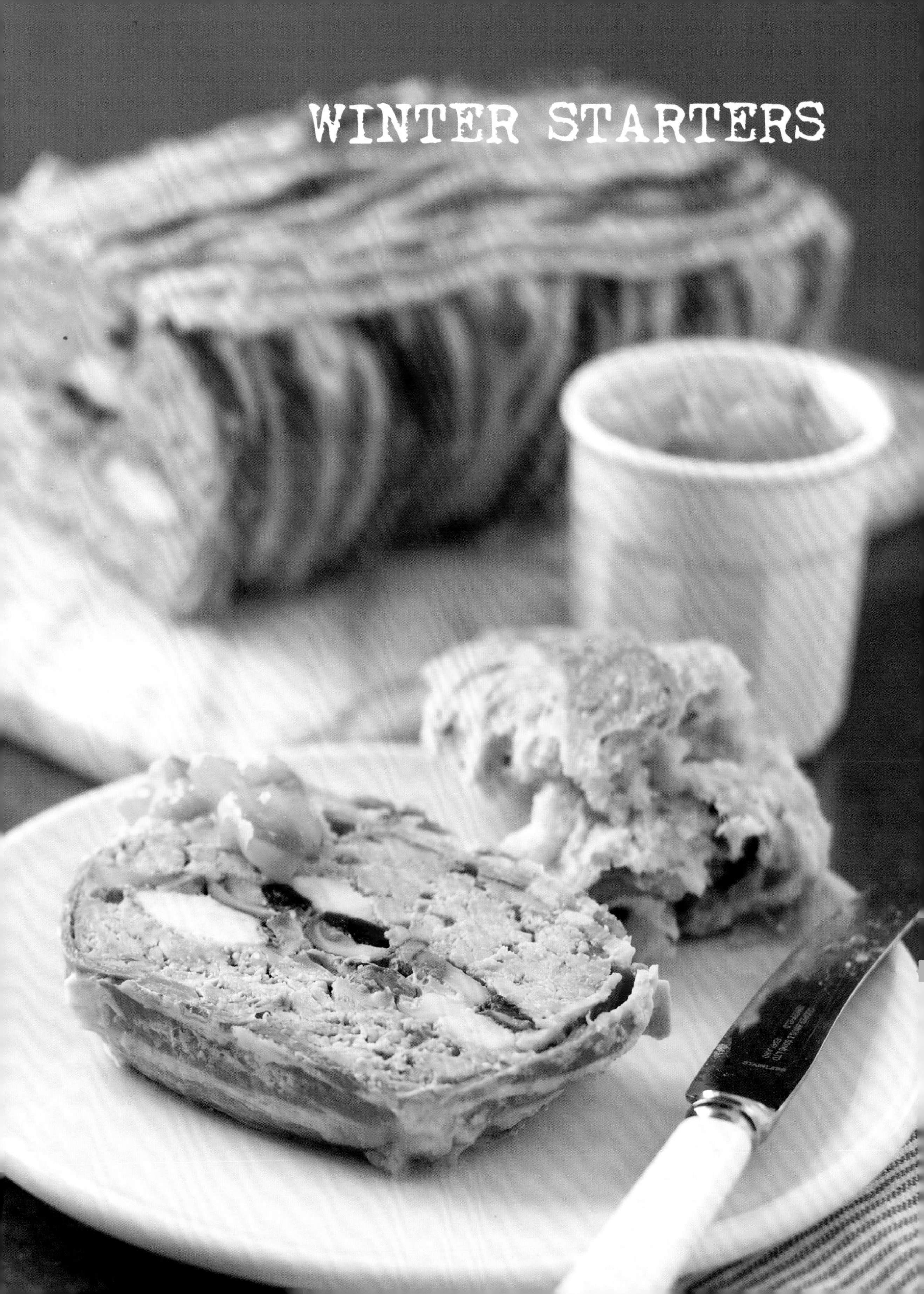

Super-quick salmon pâté

This is so zippy, it's almost cheating: chopped smoked salmon, horseradish, herbs and a dash of heat for a bit of edge, and hey presto, a comforting and tasty protein fix in a flash. More dash than cash? Use smoked salmon trimmings – they cost a fraction of the sliced variety.

prep 10 mins **cook** 2 mins SERVES 6

ingredients

250g smoked salmon
250g cream cheese
4 tbsp crème fraîche
1 tbsp creamed horseradish
Juice of ½ lemon, plus extra
    wedges to serve
2 shallots, finely chopped
½ small bunch chives, snipped
1 tbsp freshly chopped flat-
    leaf parsley
A few drops of Tabasco
Salt and freshly ground black
    pepper
Bread, such as baguette
Cornichons and caperberries

1 Finely slice the smoked salmon and put it in a bowl with the cream cheese, crème fraîche, horseradish, lemon juice, shallots, chives, parsley and Tabasco. Stir everything together to make a pâté and season. Spoon into small jars and chill.

2 Slice the bread into very thin slices and toast until just golden. Divide among six plates, put a jar of pâté on each, and add a spoonful of cornichons and caperberries. Serve with wedges of lemon.

"If you don't like lumps in your pâté, tip the smoked salmon and cheese into a food processor and blend it until it's just smooth. Scrape it into a bowl and stir in all the other ingredients."

Rich and warming root vegetable soup

This soup is a meal in itself. Celeriac and parsnip are two of winter's best root vegetables, rich in flavour and with a texture that warms the cockles of the heart.

prep 10 mins **cook** 25 mins SERVES 6

ingredients

25g butter
1 tsp olive oil
1 onion, chopped
2 garlic cloves, chopped
1 small potato, roughly chopped
1 celeriac, roughly chopped
2 parsnips, roughly chopped
2 tsp fennel or cumin seeds
1 litre hot chicken or vegetable
    stock
Salt and freshly ground black
    pepper
6-8 tbsp double cream
Squeeze of lemon juice
Root vegetable crisps, to
    garnish
Handful of parsley, finely
    chopped

1 Put the butter and olive oil in a pan and heat gently until the butter has melted. Add the onion and cook for 15 minutes over a low heat until softened. Stir in the garlic and cook for 1 minute.

2 Add the potato, celeriac, parsnips and seeds, and give everything a good stir to coat in the buttery onion mixture. Pour in half the stock, season well, then cover and simmer over a gentle heat until the vegetables are really tender.

3 Cool the mixture and purée in a food processor or liquidiser until smooth. Return to the pan, adding the rest of the stock to give the desired thickness. Warm gently until hot.

4 Stir in the double cream and lemon juice. Season to taste, ladle into bowls and serve with root vegetable crisps and a sprinkling of parsley.

"This soup freezes brilliantly. Make up to the end of Step 3, then cool and freeze in a freezer-proof container for up to three months. To enjoy, thaw overnight at a cool room temperature, then complete the recipe."

Gougère buns with creamy mushrooms

These savoury choux buns, flavoured with cheese and filled with creamy mushrooms, are an ideal starter. Take care when pouring in the beaten eggs – add only enough to make the mixture smooth and glossy, otherwise the gougères will end up heavy.

prep 20-30 mins **cook** 40 mins SERVES 6

ingredients

65g plain flour
50g butter, chopped
2 medium eggs, plus 1 egg yolk, beaten
Pinch of English mustard powder
Salt and freshly ground black pepper
75g Gruyère cheese, grated

For the filling
250g baby chestnut mushrooms, quartered
50g butter
3 tbsp Madeira
75ml double cream
2-3 thyme sprigs, snipped, plus extra to garnish
Salt and freshly ground black pepper
Salad, to serve

1 Preheat the oven to 200°C/180°C fan oven/gas mark 6. Line two large baking sheets with baking parchment. Sift the flour over a sheet of greaseproof paper.

2 Put the butter in a pan with 150ml water. Heat gently, bringing it to a rolling boil. Take the pan off the heat and tip in the flour from the greaseproof paper. Beat quickly until the mixture forms a paste and comes away from the sides of the pan.

3 Cool slightly. Whisk 2 whole eggs in a bowl, then gradually beat enough into the mixture until it looks smooth, glossy and shiny. Fold in the mustard, a little salt and half the cheese.

4 Spoon six mounds onto each baking sheet, spaced well apart. Brush with the beaten egg yolk and sprinkle the remaining cheese over the top. Bake for 30-35 minutes. Use a sharp knife to cut in half.

5 Meanwhile, fry the mushrooms in the butter for 4-5 minutes. Stir in the Madeira, cream and thyme, season the mixture and let it bubble for 3-4 minutes. Spoon into the warm buns, scatter over more snipped thyme leaves, and serve with salad.

Cheat's cheese fondue

This simple way of doing a cheese fondue calls for no more effort than turning on the oven and baking a whole Camembert in its box. Flavour it with any herbs you have to hand, then let the heat do the work, turning the inside into silky, molten indulgence.

prep 5 mins **cook** around 30 mins SERVES 4

ingredients

1 whole Camembert in its box
1 garlic bulb
A few sprigs of rosemary
A little olive oil
White wine
Salt and freshly ground black
    pepper
Crusty bread, to serve

1 Preheat the oven to 200°C/180°C fan oven/gas mark 6. Peel the plastic wrapping away from the cheese and then put the cheese back in its box.

2 Slice the top off the garlic bulb, then peel the bits of garlic clove that have fallen off. Make five or six holes in the top of the cheese using a sharp knife, then push the bits of garlic into the holes with a couple of sprigs of rosemary.

3 Rub the main part of the garlic bulb all over with oil, cover with foil, then bake on a baking sheet for 10-15 minutes. Spoon 2 tbsp white wine over the cheese, then season it and bake alongside the garlic for a further 10-15 minutes.

4 Serve with crusty bread.

"Any woody herbs can be used in this recipe. Don't worry if the Camembert is under-ripe – it will still come out with a deliciously oozy consistency."

No-cook smoked salmon roulade

This is a cinch – a quick-mix filling of cream cheese and brown shrimps wrapped in a blanket of fragrant smoked salmon, simply served with slices of crunchy toast and lime wedges.

prep 10 mins, plus chilling SERVES 4

ingredients

120g smoked salmon
100g cream cheese
Zest of ½ lime, plus 1 tsp lime juice
1 tbsp freshly chopped parsley
Freshly ground black pepper
100g brown shrimps
Toast and wedges of lime, to serve

1 Line a board with clingfilm, then place the smoked salmon slices on top, overlapping them, to make a rectangle measuring about 20 x 12cm.

2 Beat together the cream cheese, lime zest and juice, parsley and pepper to taste. It should be quite stiff. Gently stir in 75g of the shrimps. Spread the mixture over the first half of the length of the salmon.

3 Roll up carefully so as not to squeeze out too much filling, and wrap tightly in the clingfilm, securing the ends neatly. Chill until required or for up to two days.

4 When ready to serve, unwrap and, using a very sharp knife, cut the roulade into 12 thick slices. Arrange three pieces of roulade on each plate, spoon a few remaining shrimps over and serve with the toast and a wedge of lime for squeezing over.

"For a budget version, use slices of smoked trout instead of smoked salmon."

Caldo verde (hearty winter soup)

This is a Portuguese national favourite that translates as 'green broth' – it couldn't be simpler and yet packs a big flavour punch. The gentle spice from the chorizo and paprika provides the base flavour, while the kale and the starchy potatoes turn it into a bowl of comforting warmth.

prep 10 mins **cook** 25 mins SERVES 6

ingredients

2 tbsp olive oil
1 onion, chopped
2 garlic cloves, finely sliced
¼ tsp smoked paprika
Salt and freshly ground black
    pepper
200g cooking chorizo or smoked
    pork sausages, skin removed
    and sliced
4 large floury potatoes, such as
    Maris Piper, coarsely
    chopped
500g kale, thinly sliced
1.5 litres hot chicken stock

1 In a large pan, gently heat the oil and cook the onion for 10 minutes until starting to soften and caramelise. Stir in the garlic and paprika and cook for 2-3 minutes more. Season well.

2 Add the chorizo, potatoes and kale, and stir to coat. Cook, stirring for 5 minutes or until the kale has wilted. Add the stock and bring to the boil. Partially cover and simmer for about 20 minutes or until the potatoes are tender.

3 Serve with crusty bread.

"Don't serve this in a cold tureen: the easiest way to warm one is to fill it with boiling water for 5 minutes while the soup is cooking."

◄ WINTER STARTERS

1) **Theo Randall** is head chef at Theo Randall At The InterContinental, London. 2) During his career as author, TV chef and restaurant proprietor, **Phil Vickery** has held a Michelin star. 3) TV personality and chef **John Burton Race**. 4) **Olly Smith** is an enthusiastic TV presenter, wine expert, foodie and writer. 5) **Mark Lloyd**, chef, forager and wild food expert. 6) **Dean Edwards** is resident chef on ITV's *Lorraine*.

5

6

WINTER MAINS ▶

Mustard-crusted ribs of beef and Yorkshire pudding

Ribs of beef still on the bone, or 'standing' ribs, look magnificent but can be difficult to carve, so ask the butcher to chine the joint (cut along the backbone). Leave the mustard out of the flour crust if you like, but season it well. For a more budget-friendly joint, go for a rolled sirloin of beef – it's still tender and very tasty.

prep 5 mins **cook** 1 hour plus SERVES 8-10, WITH LEFTOVERS

ingredients

175g plain flour
1 tsp powdered mustard
Salt and freshly ground black pepper
3-rib joint of beef on the bone (or boned and rolled, if you prefer), at room temperature
2 eggs
200ml milk
A little oil

1 Preheat the oven to 220°C/200°C fan oven/gas mark 7. Mix together about 25g flour, the mustard and seasoning, and rub the mixture well over the whole joint. Transfer to a roasting tin.

2 Roast for 40 minutes, turn the heat down to 190°C/170°C fan oven/gas mark 5 and cook as follows: for rare beef, give it a further 10 minutes per kilo, then turn off the oven and leave the joint until you are ready to carve – at least 15-20 minutes. For just-pink beef, cook for a further 20 minutes per kilo, then leave the joint for at least 20-30 minutes before carving. For a well-cooked joint, allow a further 25-30 minutes per kilo and again, leave for 25-30 minutes before carving. Once cooked to your liking, place the joint on a warm platter and cover with foil to keep warm while you cook the Yorkshire puddings.

3 Turn the oven back up to 220°C/200°C fan oven/gas mark 7. Beat the eggs with the milk, then gradually beat in the remaining flour and a little salt to give a really smooth batter. Now beat in 2-3 tbsp cold water to lighten the batter. Sieve if still lumpy.

4 Drop ½ tsp oil into the holes on a 12-hole patty tin and place it in the oven until the fat is smoking. Carefully half-fill each hole with batter and return to the oven. Reduce the heat to 200°C/180°C fan oven/gas mark 6 and cook for 25-35 minutes or until well risen and golden. Serve immediately with the carved beef and gravy (see tip below).

"For gravy, leave 1-2 tbsp fat in the roasting tin. Stir in 2 tbsp plain flour. Cook for 1 minute. Add 400ml hot beef stock and a splash of red wine and stir well. Simmer for 5 mins until syrupy."

Pan-fried guinea fowl with mushroom and Madeira sauce

Originally a game bird, guinea fowl is now bred as a domestic fowl, which means we get to enjoy it all year round. It has a delicate, almost sweet flavour that's similar to chicken. Cook it on the bone in pieces for a really tender, moist result, and serve with buttered cabbage.

prep 10 mins **cook** 30 mins SERVES 4

ingredients

30g plain flour
Salt and freshly ground black pepper
1 guinea fowl
2-3 tbsp sunflower oil
2 red onions, sliced
3-4 garlic cloves, crushed
250g mixed wild mushrooms (or use 100g dried porcini soaked in the hot stock as directed)
450ml hot chicken stock
75ml Madeira

1 Place the flour in a shallow bowl and season.

2 Joint the guinea fowl into 6-8 portions: wing, leg (which can be divided into thigh and drumstick, if large enough) and breast (which can also be cut into two). See page 284 for how to joint a chicken – the same instructions apply here.

3 Heat the oil in a sauté pan with lid, and fry the onions and garlic until softened. Set aside on a plate, then fry off the portions of guinea fowl, skin-side down first, until nicely golden all over.

4 Return the onions to the pan along with the mushrooms and stock and stir gently while heating through. When the liquid is just bubbling, cover the pan and leave it to simmer gently for 15-20 minutes, or until the guinea fowl is tender. Stir occasionally to avoid sticking or burning.

5 Add the Madeira and bring to a bubble again, stirring occasionally. Transfer the guinea fowl portions to a heated serving dish and cover with foil. Give the sauce a final heat through, stirring well, and check the seasoning.

6 Divide the mushrooms between four heated plates, place the guinea fowl portions on top, and spoon over a little of the sauce, strained if you like.

"Guinea fowl is a robustly flavoured bird that lends itself to being paired with fruity flavours – cranberries work a treat, for example."

Beef rendang with coriander

Astound your guests by serving this up on the ultimate eco-friendly tableware –
a banana leaf. This is a brilliant way to enjoy the cheaper cuts of beef: cook them
long and slow, let the spices soak in, and the meat will be unbelievably tender
and flavoursome.

prep 30 mins **cook** 3 hours SERVES 4

ingredients

2 dried red chillies (or 3-4 fresh
   red chillies, seeded)
5 garlic cloves
5cm piece fresh root ginger,
   grated
1 medium onion, or 4-5
   shallots, quartered
400ml can coconut milk
2-3 tbsp vegetable oil
1 tbsp ground coriander
1 tbsp ground cumin
2-3cm cinnamon sticks,
   broken up
3 cardamom pods, seeds only
1-2 tbsp Thai red curry paste
700g stewing beef, cubed
2 tbsp light brown soft sugar
300g basmati rice
1 tsp tamarind paste or 1 tbsp
   lemon zest
Salt and freshly ground black
   pepper
1 tbsp chopped coriander, plus
   a few sprigs
Natural yoghurt, to serve

1 Place the chillies, garlic, ginger, onion and a little of the coconut
milk in a blender, and whiz to make a smooth paste.

2 Heat the oil in a large flameproof casserole and add the paste,
ground coriander, cumin, cinnamon, cardamom seeds, curry
paste and stir everything together. Cook for a few minutes
to thicken the sauce. Add the beef and stir until well coated.
Cook for 5 minutes over a medium heat until the meat has
browned.

3 Add the remaining coconut milk and the sugar and bring to
the boil. Cover and simmer very slowly over a low heat for
about 3 hours, watching it carefully, until the meat is tender.
Stir occasionally to check the meat doesn't stick.

4 About half an hour before the curry is ready, cook the basmati
rice according to the packet instructions.

5 When the meat is really tender, stir in the tamarind paste
(or lemon zest), season to taste and stir in the chopped
coriander. Garnish with the coriander sprigs. and serve with
the rice and the yoghurt.

"This is a Southeast Asian-
style dry curry – the sauce
is supposed to be reduced
down and caramelised to a
thickness that just coats
the meat."

Auntie Barb's sausage pie

This recipe has been immortalised by a terrific cook known to her friends and family in East London as 'Auntie Barb'. It couldn't be quicker or easier, as it uses ready-made pastry and sausage meat and there's no need to serve it with any accompaniments – it's utterly delicious on its own, hot or cold!

prep 20 minutes **cook** 45-50 minutes SERVES 10

ingredients

500g pack shortcrust pastry
A little plain flour
500g good-quality pork sausage meat, or the same quantity of well-flavoured sausages
2 medium eggs
1 onion, chopped finely
1 tbsp freshly chopped herbs, such as parsley, sage or thyme
Salt and freshly ground black pepper

1 Preheat the oven to 190°C/170°C fan oven/gas mark 5. Put a baking sheet in the oven to heat up.

2 Cut about two-thirds off the pack of pastry and roll it out on a clean work surface or board sprinkled with a little plain flour. Use it to line a deep, fluted 20-22cm loose-bottomed flan tin.

3 Put the sausage meat in a bowl (if using sausages, squeeze out of the casing into the bowl). Beat 1 of the eggs and add to the bowl with the onion and herbs. Season, and mix everything together. Spoon into the pastry case.

4 Roll out the remaining pastry to 2-3mm thick, and make a round big enough to cover the tin. Place it on top, then roll a rolling pin over the top to cut off the excess pastry. Crimp the edges together. Beat the remaining egg and brush over the top.

5 Cut out the letters for 'sausage pie', place on top and glaze again. Bake in the oven for 45-50 minutes until golden brown. Allow to cool for 5 minutes, then push out of the tin onto a board, slice and serve.

"Don't just stick to pork - ring the changes with venison or beef sausages instead."

Moussaka

Originally an Arab dish, it was eventually adopted by the Greeks. Its layers of roasted aubergine and spicy meat mix topped with cheese sauce are bursting with Mediterranean flavour, but it's the health-giving aubergine that's the real star of the show. What we care most about, though, is that it's totally delicious.

prep 1 hour **cook** 30-45 mins approx., plus standing SERVES 6-8

ingredients

2 aubergines, sliced into rounds
2 tbsp olive oil, plus extra for
   brushing
750g beef, lamb or pork mince
1 large onion, finely chopped
2 garlic cloves, crushed
½ tsp ground cinnamon
1 sprig fresh rosemary
2 sprigs fresh thyme
2 x 400g cans plum tomatoes
Salt and freshly ground black
   pepper

For the cheese sauce
40g butter
40g plain flour
600ml milk
Freshly grated nutmeg
2 egg yolks
75g mature Cheddar, grated

1 Preheat the oven to 200°C/180°C fan oven/gas mark 6. Brush the rounds of aubergine with oil and place on an oiled baking sheet. Bake in the oven for 20-30 minutes until just golden.

2 While the aubergines are cooking, brown the mince in a pan in batches until golden. Spoon into a bowl.

3 Drain any fat from the pan and return it to the heat. Add the olive oil and sauté the onion and garlic over a gentle heat for about 10 minutes until starting to soften. Stir in the cinnamon and fresh herbs (no need to chop the herbs – just drop in whole sprigs, and pull out the stalks once cooked, leaving behind the fragrant leaves).

4 Return the mince to the pan with the tomatoes, using the back of a wooden spoon to break them down. Season well, cover, bring to a simmer and cook for 40-50 minutes until tender.

5 Meanwhile, make the cheese sauce. Melt the butter in a pan and stir in the flour. Cook for 1 minute until bubbling. Slide the pan off the heat and slowly stir in the milk. Return to the heat and bring to the boil, stirring all the time. Simmer for 2-3 minutes until thickened.

6 Cool the sauce a little, then season with nutmeg, salt and pepper and stir in the egg yolks and half the cheese.

7 Create alternating layers of mince and aubergine in a large ovenproof dish, finishing with a layer of aubergines. Spoon over the sauce, then sprinkle with the remaining cheese.

8 Reduce the oven temperature to 180°C/160°C fan oven/gas mark 4. Bake the moussaka for around 30-45 minutes until golden on top. Allow to stand for 15 minutes before serving.

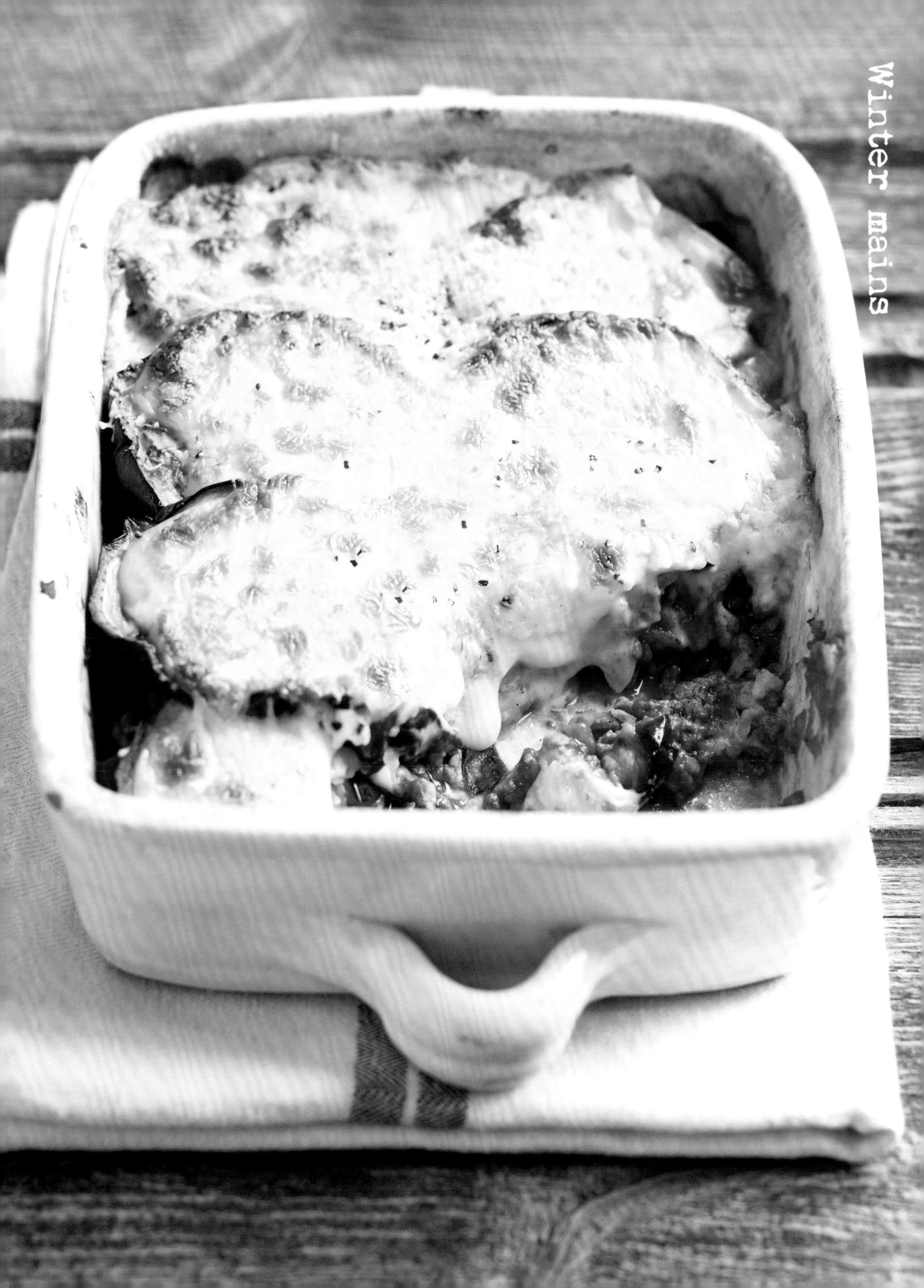

Braised lamb shanks with beans and herbs

There's a rustic charm about this dish — it's full of flavour and tastes even better the longer you cook it. The end result is deliciously tender.

prep 30 mins **cook** 2 hours SERVES 4

ingredients

A little olive oil
2 onions, sliced
4 meaty lamb shanks
300ml each white wine and hot
  chicken stock
1 tbsp Worcestershire sauce
2-3 large garlic cloves
400g can chopped tomatoes
Several sprigs rosemary
400g can of flageolet, haricot or
  lima beans
A few sprigs of sage, chopped
Salt and freshly ground black
  pepper

1 Heat a little oil in a large ovenproof and heatproof casserole with lid, and sauté the onions for around 10 minutes over a low-to-medium heat until just turning golden. Transfer with a draining spoon to a small plate.

2 Add the shanks to the hot pan and brown on all sides, adding more oil if necessary. When the lamb is a good colour, return the onions to the pan and add the wine, stock, Worcestershire sauce, garlic, tomatoes and rosemary. Cover and simmer very gently for about 1 hour or until the meat is tender, but not yet falling off the bone.

3 Add the drained beans (reserving their liquor) and the sage, and season. Cover, bring back to the boil and cook until the meat is really tender and the liquid has reduced.

4 Check the seasoning and add a few more sage leaves and some of the bean liquor if the dish is to sit for some time. Cover and keep warm until ready to serve.

"Serve with creamy mashed potatoes and lightly steamed, buttered cabbage for a hearty winter supper."

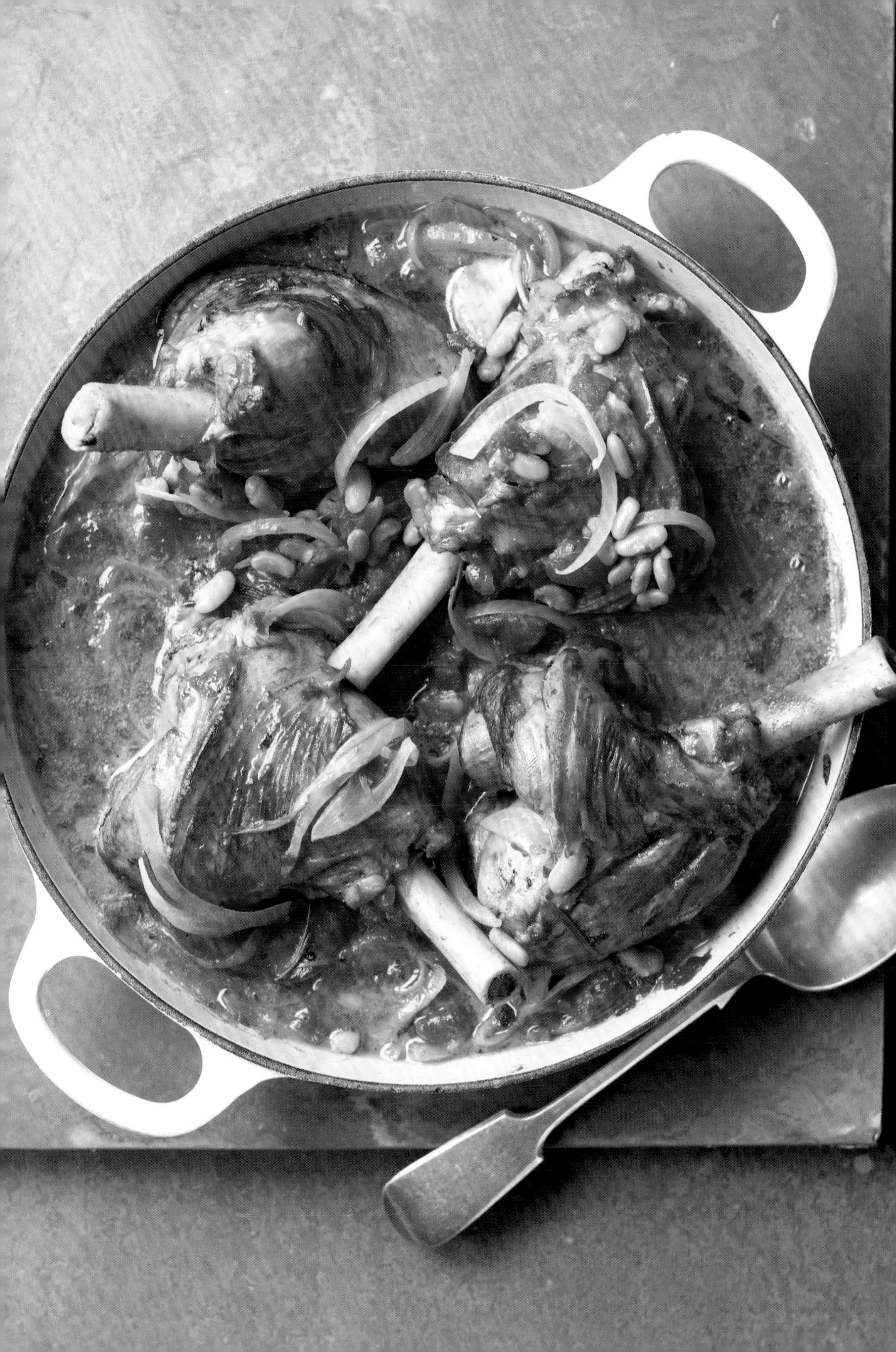

GET READY FOR CHRISTMAS

Buy your Brussels sprouts on the stalk, as this is the freshest you'll find them, and then make sure you keep them in a cool place away from the central heating.

MORE WINTER MAINS ▶

No-fuss Christmas turkey

This is the ultimate in hassle-free Christmas cooking. Roasting a turkey is just like doing a chicken, only it's three times bigger. Don't skimp on quality – a good bird will not only taste delicious, it will reward you with rich juices for the gravy. To stuff the turkey, fill only the neck cavity so that the heat can penetrate right through the main body of the bird while it's cooking.

prep 30 mins **cook** around 4 hours SERVES 8, WITH LEFTOVERS

ingredients

4.5kg turkey, at room
   temperature, with giblets
2 onions, quartered
1 celery stick, cut into three
1 carrot, cut into three
1 bay leaf
1 lemon, quartered
55g butter, melted, plus extra
   for greasing
Salt and freshly ground black
   pepper

For the gravy
2 tbsp plain flour
150ml dry white wine

Carving the turkey

To carve, take a tip from Paul Kelly of Kelly Bronze Turkeys: take a sharp carving knife and remove the wings. Hold the leg and carve between the thigh and the body, moving down through the bone to remove it. Carve down the breast bone, keeping the knife close to the bone to remove the meat. Slice across the grain to make thin slices, and transfer to a warm platter. Next, carve the meat from the thigh and leg and, with the wing, place on a platter. Do the same on the other side of the turkey, if needed.

1 Preheat the oven to 230°C/210°C fan oven/gas mark 8. Put the turkey giblets in a pan with 600ml water, 1 quartered onion, the celery, carrot and the bay leaf. Bring to the boil and simmer for 20 minutes. Set aside to cool.

2 Wipe the turkey dry with kitchen paper. Place the remaining onion and the lemon inside it. Rub the skin with melted butter and season inside the cavity and all over the bird. Transfer to a large flameproof roasting tin and pour 600ml water into it.

3 Butter a piece of foil large enough to cover the turkey and seal it into the roasting tin. Roast for 1 hour without opening. Reduce the oven temperature to 170°C/150°C fan oven/gas mark 3 for a further 2½-3 hours.

4 At this stage remove the foil or fold it back, and baste the turkey with the juices. Check to see if it's cooked by pushing a metal skewer into the thickest part of the thigh. If the juices still run pink, baste it again and cook for a further 20 minutes.

5 Remove from the oven. Transfer the turkey to a warm serving platter, cover tightly with foil and two clean tea towels to keep it warm, and set aside to rest in a warm place.

6 Pour the juices into a large bowl and put the roasting tin back on the heat. Spoon 2 tbsp fat from the juices and put back into the roasting tin with the flour (skim off any remaining fat from the juices and discard). Stir over a medium heat for a couple of minutes, then gradually stir in the wine. Bring to the boil and allow to bubble for a couple of minutes to cook off the alcohol.

7 Slowly start to add the remaining turkey juices and the turkey stock and bring to a simmer. Cook for 5 minutes to thicken and season well. Transfer to a serving jug and take to the table with the turkey and carve.

Wine tip

Try a Marlborough Pinot Noir from New Zealand, or a white Californian Chardonnay.

All the trimmings

Here you have it: the all-singing, all-dancing Christmas extravaganza, complete with everything you need to make turkey part of a serious feast – and all in one place for easy reference.

SERVES 8

Crispy roast potatoes guaranteed

Peel and chop 1.5kg floury potatoes, such as Maris Piper, into chunks. Put in a large pan of boiling salted water and bring to the boil. Simmer for around 5 minutes. Drain well, return to the pan and give the potatoes a good shake. Sprinkle them with 1½ tbsp plain flour, toss again and season well. Put 3 tbsp goose fat (or olive oil if you're cooking for vegetarians) into a roasting tin and place in an oven preheated to 200°C/180°C fan oven/ gas mark 6. As soon as the fat has melted and is hot, add the potatoes and toss so they're all coated in the oil. Roast for 1-1½ hours until golden and crispy. Season with salt and serve.

Brussels sprouts with nutmeg butter

Mix 50g softened butter in a bowl with salt, freshly ground black pepper and plenty of freshly grated nutmeg. Steam 600g Brussels sprouts in a pan until just tender. Return to the pan and add the butter. Cover and give the pan a good shake – its heat will melt the butter and coat the Brussels sprouts.

How to make turkey crackling "Paul Kelly, who rears Kelly Bronze turkeys, is a big fan of using the turkey skin to make crackling. Here's how to do it. Remove the skin from the cooked bird. Lay it on a lipped baking sheet and roast in the oven once the turkey is resting. Cook for 10-15 minutes at around 200°C/180°C fan oven/gas mark 6, until it's crisp."

(continued...)

Roast parsnips

Heat 2 tbsp olive oil in a roasting tin preheated to 200°C/180°C fan oven/gas mark 6. Peel and halve 1kg parsnips lengthways. Cut out and remove the core from any large vegetables and put in the heated roasting tin. Season well and toss to coat. Roast for 45-50 minutes until golden and tender.

Steamed carrots with a lemon dressing

Whisk together 2 tbsp extra virgin olive oil, 1 tbsp white wine vinegar and zest of ¼ lemon. Season well. Peel and chop 750g carrots into rounds or batons. Steam until tender, drain the water, return them to the pan and add the dressing. Toss everything together and serve garnished with thyme.

Braised red cabbage

Cut 1 red cabbage through the middle. Chop out and discard the core. Finely shred the cabbage and layer up in a large flameproof casserole with the following ingredients: 1 large finely sliced onion, 2 peeled, cored and finely chopped Bramley apples, 2 tbsp light brown soft sugar, 2 tbsp red wine vinegar. Scatter with a good pinch of ground cloves and freshly grated nutmeg. Dot with 15g butter, pour in 100ml water, and season well. Cover and bring to the boil. Turn the heat to its lowest setting and cook very slowly for about 2 hours, stirring every now and then. This can also be made up to a month ahead and frozen. Thaw overnight and reheat on the day with a splash of boiling water if the mixture seems a little dry.

What to do with Christmas leftovers "These taste just as delicious the following day as they did on the day itself."

Bubble and squeak

Slice the Brussels sprouts thinly and chop the potatoes and carrots. Pan-fry them with a knob of butter and a drizzle of oil, mashing everything down with a wooden spoon. Add shredded turkey or ham, and serve with a poached or fried egg on top.

Christmas roast soup

Put leftover Brussels sprouts, chopped carrots and potatoes in a pan with some chicken or vegetable stock. Add any leftover gravy. Bring up to the boil and simmer for 5 minutes, then cool and whiz in a blender. Top with shredded turkey and a small spoonful of cranberry sauce. (Add red cabbage if you dare, but it does turn the soup a slightly unfortunate shade of blue-grey!)

(continued...)

Best-ever chestnut stuffing

Melt 25g butter in a pan and sauté 1 finely chopped onion until soft. Tip into a bowl to cool. Add 350g good-quality skinned sausages, 100g breadcrumbs (or use a ready-made dried stuffing mix), 175g cooked and chopped chestnuts, zest and juice of 1 lemon, a large handful of chopped parsley, 1 tsp dried sage and 1 beaten egg. Mix well. Roll into balls. Once the turkey is out of the oven, increase the temperature to 200°C/180°C fan oven/ gas mark 6. Heat a roasting tin with 2 tbsp vegetable oil. Add the balls and roast for 30-40 minutes, turning halfway through. Garnish with thyme. Alternatively, put the mixture into a roasting tin and cook as before.

Cranberry and orange relish

Put 300g cranberries (or frozen and defrosted) into a pan with the zest and juice of 1 orange, a pinch of ground cloves, 75g each sultanas and caster sugar. Heat gently, stirring to dissolve the sugar. Cover and bring to the boil. Simmer for 5 minutes.

Creamy bread sauce

Pour 600ml full-fat milk into a pan. Peel and quarter 1 onion, then stud each quarter with 2-3 cloves. Add to the pan with 2 bay leaves. Bring up to the boil, then turn down the heat and simmer gently for 10 minutes. Remove from the heat and set aside for 30 minutes. Strain into a pan and bring to a simmer. Stir in 150g fresh breadcrumbs, simmer for 3 minutes and then swirl in 50g butter and 50ml double cream. Season with salt, freshly ground black pepper and a grating of nutmeg.

Pigs in blankets

Cut 6 rashers streaky bacon in half. Use the back of a knife to stretch each piece on a board, then wrap each around 12 chipolatas. Roast in the oven at 200°C/180°C fan oven/ gas mark 6 for 25-30 minutes until golden and cooked through.

"Cranberry sauce and bread sauce can be cooked up to two days in advance, or frozen for up to a month. Stuffing balls and pigs in blankets can both be prepared up to two days in advance."

Whisky and maple glazed ham

This majestic joint, studded with aromatic cloves, is a must-have at Christmas. The smart way of making the most of it is to serve it hot on Christmas Eve, then let it cool and serve the remainder on Boxing Day with the leftover turkey. It demands something crisp and crunchy on the side, so try the knock-up-in-minutes coleslaw recipe in the tip below.

prep 20 mins **cook** 5 hours SERVES 6

ingredients

5.5kg gammon on the bone
1 onion, quartered
2 celery sticks, roughly chopped
A bunch of fresh woody herbs,
    such as rosemary or thyme
1 tsp black peppercorns,
    roughly crushed
A handful of cloves
2 tbsp mixed spice
125g maple syrup
125ml whisky

1 Put the gammon into a very large pan, and add enough cold water to cover, then bring to the boil. Tip away this water and pour in as much fresh cold water again to cover. Add the onion, celery, herbs and peppercorns and bring to the boil. Turn the heat down low and simmer for 4 hours, skimming off the scum every now and then.

2 Strain the stock and reserve, then leave the ham to cool until you can touch it comfortably. Peel away the skin, leaving a thin layer of fat behind. Score the fat into diamonds, sticking in a clove where the lines cross.

3 Preheat the oven to 190°C/170°C fan oven/gas mark 5. Sit the ham on a rack in a large roasting tin and pour in about 2.5cm of the reserved stock (use any leftover stock for soup). Mix the spice, maple syrup and whisky together, then brush a little over the ham. Bake for 45 minutes to 1 hour, brushing with the rest of the glaze every 20 minutes.

Wine tip
Rioja Reserva Crozes-Hermitage will balance these flavours beautifully.

"Serve with apple and hazelnut coleslaw. Peel, core and roughly grate the apples into a bowl. Stir in the juice of 1 lemon. Finely shred 225g white cabbage, then finely chop 2 shallots. Add to the apple with 25g chopped hazelnuts and 2 tbsp mayonnaise. Season and toss well before serving."

Kedgeree – the classic New Year brunch

After a long night, this is the perfect morning-after-the-night-before restorative. The rice provides energy-giving carbohydrate, while the fish and eggs are rich in protein and B vitamins. Health creds aside, it's also great for feeding a crowd: just multiply the ingredients as required, serve on a platter and let everyone dig in.

prep 10 mins **cook** 25 mins SERVES 4

ingredients

2 large eggs
2 tbsp olive oil
1 medium onion, finely chopped
1 tsp mild or medium curry powder
1 tsp ground turmeric
200g basmati rice
450ml hot chicken or vegetable stock
500g smoked haddock, skinned
2-3 tbsp milk
25g butter
Salt and freshly ground black pepper
Fresh parsley sprigs, to serve
Paprika

1. Put the eggs in a pan of cold water. Bring to the boil and cook for 7 minutes. Place them in a bowl of cold water and set aside.

2. Heat the oil in a pan over a low heat and cook the onions with the spices for about 10 minutes until softened.

3. Stir the rice into the onion mixture to coat it in the spices, then pour in the stock. Cover with a lid and bring to a gentle boil. Turn down the heat and cook for 10-12 minutes, or according to the timing on the pack.

4. While the rice is cooking, put the fish in a pan with the 2-3 tbsp milk and simmer gently until it is just cooked and separates into big chunks. Pick out any bones and stir the chunks of fish and juices into the rice mixture.

5. Stir the butter into the mixture and season well. Keep the pan over a medium heat so that the rice stays heated through, stirring every now and then to stop it sticking.

6. Peel the eggs and cut into halves or quarters. Spoon the rice mixture into a serving bowl, top with the eggs, parsley and a dusting of paprika, and serve immediately.

"Microwaving fish keeps it wonderfully moist, so you could just put the haddock in a microwavable dish with the milk, cover with clingfilm, and cook on high for 3-4 minutes until it flakes easily."

Warm clementines with brandy syrup

Let's face it, not everyone is mad about Christmas pudding — this is a lighter, less indulgent alternative, which you can either whip up in minutes or make ahead and store in the fridge for up to three days before serving.

prep 15 mins **cook** 7 mins SERVES 6

ingredients

12 clementines
50g butter
4 tbsp light muscovado sugar
Juice of 4 oranges
125ml brandy
Greek yoghurt, to serve

1 Peel the clementines and take off all the white pith from the skin. Cut each in half through the equator.

2 Melt the butter in a shallow sauté pan, then stir in the sugar, orange juice and brandy. Bring to the boil and continue to cook for 2 minutes.

3 Add the peeled clementines and cook in batches for about 5 minutes, turning halfway through. Keep spooning the sauce over the fruit as it cooks, then transfer to a serving dish. Serve warm with Greek yoghurt.

Orange mincemeat tarts

Classic, crumbly mince pies made with a smidgen of orange and served with a sweet orange butter are to sigh for. The cornflour in the pastry helps make the cases super-light. Make plenty and freeze ahead of the Christmas rush – family and friends will motor through plate-loads of them.

prep 40 mins **cook** 20 mins MAKES AROUND 18 TARTS

ingredients

200g plain flour
25g cornflour
25g icing sugar, plus extra for dusting
Pinch of salt
150g chilled unsalted butter, cut into cubes
1 egg yolk
1-2 tbsp iced water
6-8 tbsp mincemeat (or make your own – see recipe below)
1 tsp grated orange zest
1 tbsp orange juice
Milk, for brushing

1 Sieve the flours and icing sugar together into a bowl with the salt. Gently rub in the butter using your fingertips until the mixture resembles breadcrumbs. Blend the egg yolk with the 1-2 tbsp iced water in a small bowl and stir into the flour mixture using a table knife until it looks crumbly and is starting to come together. You can do these stages in a food processor, too – just take care not to overprocess the mixture when you add the egg and water.

2 Bring together with your hands to make a firm dough. Knead lightly on a floured board until smooth. Wrap and chill for 15-20 minutes.

3 Roll out the dough on a lightly floured surface to 3mm thick and cut out 12 x 7.5cm circles and 12 stars using a 6mm star-cutter for the tops. Place the round bases into each tartlet tin and prick them once or twice. You'll have enough pastry left over to make around six more pies.

4 Mix the mincemeat with the 1 tsp grated orange zest and the 1 tbsp orange juice. Preheat the oven to 190°C/170°C fan oven/gas mark 5. Place a teaspoonful of mincemeat into each pastry case. Brush the edges with milk and top with a star. Brush with more milk, and bake for 15-20 minutes or until golden. Cool a little, then transfer to a wire rack. Dust with icing sugar. Voilà!

"For the mincemeat, soak in a bowl overnight 75g each sultanas, currants and raisins, 50g each chopped, dried apricots and dried figs or dates, 30g muscovado sugar, 50ml brandy and 1 tsp ground mixed spice. Add 2 tbsp marmalade then whiz half in a food processor until smooth. Stir it back into the remaining soaked fruit and put in a sterilised jar."

Best-ever Christmas pudding

Did you know that there's a day traditionally reserved for making your Christmas pudding? It's called 'Stir-up Sunday' – the last Sunday before Advent begins. This recipe is a carefully balanced combination of fruit, sweetness and richness from the suet. If you prefer, you can also use the same quantity of butter to replace the suet – just chill it until firm, then grate it.

prep 15 mins, plus soaking **cook** 5 hours, plus 2 hours extra SERVES 8

ingredients

A little butter, for greasing
150g each sultanas and raisins
50g chopped candied peel
50g dried figs, chopped into
     small pieces
50g glacé cherries
25g flaked almonds
100ml brandy
1 tsp mixed spice
75g dark brown soft sugar
75g shredded suet
100g breadcrumbs
Zest of 1 orange
3 medium eggs, beaten

For the whisky cream
75ml whisky
50g golden caster sugar
300ml double cream

1 Butter a pudding basin, with a volume of around 900g.

2 Put the sultanas, raisins, candied peel, dried figs, glacé cherries and flaked almonds in a large bowl and pour over the brandy. Leave to soak for an hour or so.

3 Add the mixed spice, sugar, suet, breadcrumbs, orange zest and eggs, then stir all the ingredients until the mixture is well combined.

4 Spoon into the prepared pudding basin and smooth the top. Cover the top of the pudding with a circle of baking parchment, then cover the whole pudding basin in a piece of pleated foil. Secure with string and make a handle so that it's easy to lift out once it's steamed.

5 Steam in a pan over a low heat for 5 hours, making sure the water is just bubbling and doesn't boil dry. Cool.

6 To serve, steam the pudding in a pan, as before, for 2 hours. Just before serving, put the whisky in a pan with the golden caster sugar. Bring to the boil and simmer for a couple of minutes to cook off the alcohol. Cool. Whip the cream until just thick. Stir in the whisky mixture and serve.

Wine tip
Choose an intense, dark and figgy PX sherry, or the Australian Rutherglen Muscat, both of which perfectly complement Christmas pudding.

"The whisky cream can also be made into a hot, runny sauce. Prepare the whisky and sugar as above in a pan. Pour the cream into the pan and bring to the boil. Stir well to incorporate everything, then take off the heat and serve with the pudding."

Panforte

Panforte is Italian for 'strong bread' and it dates back to the Crusaders. It's rich, fruity and nutty, and not a bread at all – 'strong' just refers to its spicy flavour. Make double, keep one for yourself, then do as the Italians do with the other one – wrap it to give to your hosts when you go visiting over the festive season.

prep 30 mins **cook** 35 mins SERVES 10-12

ingredients

15g unsalted butter, plus a little extra for greasing
Rice paper
50g dark chocolate, at least 70% cocoa solids, broken into pieces
100g blanched hazelnuts
150g whole blanched almonds
50g pine nuts
50g candied peel, finely chopped
125g ready-to-eat dried figs, finely chopped
Zest of 1 orange
75g plain flour, sifted
1 tsp ground cinnamon
Pinch of ground black pepper, mace and nutmeg
75ml sweet sherry
5-6 tbsp thick-set honey
150g golden caster sugar

1 Grease a 20cm round springform cake tin and line with baking parchment. Cut a round of rice paper to fit, and place it on top of the parchment. Preheat the oven to 150°C/130°C fan oven/gas mark 2.

2 Put the chocolate in a bowl with the butter and place in the microwave for 30-60 seconds on low until melted. Check the bowl every now and then and tip it around to ensure the pieces of chocolate melt evenly. Stir gently to mix, then set aside to cool a little.

3 Whiz the hazelnuts and almonds in a food processor to roughly chop them. (Or chop them by hand with a large sharp knife in batches on a board.) Place in a large bowl with the pine nuts, candied peel and figs.

4 Stir the orange zest, flour, cinnamon and spices into the nut mixture. Put the sherry, honey and sugar together in a pan and place over a low heat. Simmer gently to dissolve the sugar. Bring to the boil and cook for 4-5 minutes to cook off the alcohol and thicken the mixture slightly. Pour into the nut mixture, along with the melted chocolate and butter and mix until well blended.

5 Spoon the mixture into the tin and spread out evenly, smoothing over the top. Bake for 30 minutes. Remove from the oven and leave to cool in the tin. The mixture may still look runny, but it will set on cooling.

6 When ready to serve, undo the lock on the springform tin, take off the parchment and slide onto a board. Slice into wedges, arrange on a plate, and enjoy.

Chocolate roulade

This moist, chocolatey and incredibly light pudding can be made ahead and chilled for up to six hours. Take it out of the fridge around half an hour before serving – allowing it to come to room temperature will release the flavours.

prep 25 mins **cook** 20 mins SERVES 6

ingredients

6 free range eggs, separated
½ tsp vanilla extract
225g caster sugar
50g cocoa powder, twice sifted
30g dark chocolate, finely
  grated
Icing sugar, sifted

For the filling
300ml double cream
A little icing sugar, sifted

1 Preheat the oven to 180°C/160°C fan oven/gas mark 4. Line a Swiss roll tin measuring 33 x 21cm with non-stick baking parchment.

2 Whisk the egg yolks, vanilla and sugar in a large bowl until pale and fluffy and the mixture feels thick. Fold in the cocoa with a large metal spoon.

3 Whisk the egg whites in a clean, grease-free bowl until stiff peaks form. Fold one spoonful into the cocoa mixture to loosen, then fold in the remaining egg white using firm, fast strokes. Spoon into the prepared tin and spread gently and evenly into the corners.

4 Bake in the preheated oven for 20 minutes, until golden brown and springy to the touch. Leave to rest for a few minutes, then turn onto a sheet of baking parchment sprinkled with icing sugar and roll up from the shortest end, enclosing the paper. Leave until cool enough to handle – about 20 minutes – but don't leave until it's really cold or it won't roll again easily.

5 Whip the cream until just thick, then fold in the icing sugar – it will thicken more at this stage, so take care not to overwhip. Unroll the roulade carefully onto a board and sprinkle the surface with the dark chocolate and spread the whipped cream all over. Use a sharp knife to cut about 1cm into the roulade on one of the short edges (this helps to roll it up evenly), then roll up firmly. Slide onto a serving plate with the join underneath. Don't worry if the surface cracks – it usually does, and it looks all the more natural and appealing for it.

Chocolate mousse

Darkly decadent and yet lighter than air, this is the ideal ending for a special dinner. The recipe uses simple flavourings of vanilla and brandy, but if you prefer, use orange zest and match it with a citrus liqueur such as Cointreau, for a twist.

prep 20 mins, plus chilling SERVES 6

ingredients

250g good dark chocolate, at
    least 70% cocoa solids
Knob of butter
6 medium eggs, separated
A few drops of vanilla essence
50g caster sugar
3 tbsp warm brandy or hot
    black coffee
Thin crisp biscuits, such as
    almond thins, to serve,

1 Break the chocolate into small pieces and place in a small bowl with the butter. Place the bowl over a pan of simmering water, making sure the base doesn't touch the water, and allow the chocolate to melt slowly.

2 Whisk the egg yolks, vanilla and sugar together in a bowl until fluffy and light, then whisk in the warm brandy and continue to beat for 1 minute. Gently blend this warm egg mixture into the melted chocolate and allow it to cool slightly.

3 Whisk the egg whites in a clean, grease-free bowl and fold a spoonful into the chocolate mixture to loosen it. Fold in the remaining whites. Divide between six coffee cups and chill for 2 hours. Place each cup on a saucer, tuck a biscuit on the side, and serve.

"Save time and energy by microwaving the chocolate. Put it in a microwavable bowl and cook on low in 30-second bursts, checking the chocolate at the end of each time slot. Nudge unmelted pieces to the bottom of the bowl to ensure the chocolate melts evenly, but don't stir, otherwise it may stiffen into a thick mass."

Rich Parmesan cheese biscuits

Often referred to as Sablé biscuits, these savoury nibbles were first rustled up in Sablé-sur-Sarthe in 1670, according to the diaries of French aristocrat, the Marquise de Sévigné. They taste totally out of this world – with or without a drink in the other hand.

prep 20 mins **cook** 30 mins MAKES AROUND 40 BISCUITS

ingredients

150g plain flour
75g fine oatmeal or cornmeal
A generous pinch of salt
1 tsp baking powder
110g butter
40g Parmesan cheese, freshly grated
1 tsp dried oregano
A good pinch of coarsely ground black pepper
Cayenne pepper, sesame seeds, poppy seeds

1 Preheat the oven to 200°C/180°C fan oven/gas mark 6. Line two baking sheets with baking parchment.

2 Put the flour, oatmeal or cornmeal, salt and baking powder into a bowl. Rub in the butter to make fine breadcrumbs (you can also do this stage in a food processor).

3 Add the cheese, oregano and black pepper and stir in (or whiz it again). Stir in 2-3 tbsp cold water (or tip into a bowl if you've used a processor). Work the mixture together with your hands to make a dough that's pliable, but not soft. Wrap and chill for 10 minutes.

4 Roll out half the dough on a floured surface to about 4mm thick and cut about 20 biscuits of whatever shape you prefer (we used a 3cm star cutter and 3cm and 5cm round cutters). Do the same with the remaining dough. Sprinkle the stars with cayenne pepper, then roll the small round biscuits in poppy seeds and the large biscuits in sesame seeds.

5 Cook the biscuits in batches. Place half on the prepared baking sheets and bake for about 5 minutes, then reduce the heat to 170°C/150°C fan oven/gas mark 3 and continue for a further 10 minutes or until crisp and just colouring at the edges. Cool on racks. Repeat for remaining biscuits. Store in an airtight container for up to five days, or wrap well in clingfilm and freeze for up to a month. Allow 1 hour to thaw before serving.

HOW TO...

How to choose and store fresh produce

ROOT AND UNDERGROUND VEGETABLES

beetroot, carrots, celeriac, horseradish, Jerusalem artichokes, leeks and onions, parsnips, potatoes, radish, salsify, swede, turnip

How to choose
Look for unblemished, firm, deeply coloured root vegetables with no sign of sprouting, and opt for unwashed veg if you have the choice, as they'll keep better and often have more flavour. Lumps and bumps are fine, but if you're going to peel them, smooth specimens will make your life easier and minimise wastage.

How to store
Dirty root vegetables and the onion family (with the exception of spring onions, which should be refrigerated) will keep well in a paper bag in a cool room – just take off any leaves from the top first. Keep potatoes in the dark to prevent sprouting, and discard any that look greenish. Ready-scrubbed or peeled root veg should be kept in the fridge, especially in warmer weather.

ABOVE-THE-GROUND VEGETABLES

artichokes, asparagus, aubergines, beans, broccoli, Brussels sprouts, cabbage, cauliflower, courgettes and marrow, cucumber, fennel, kale and chard, peas, peppers, rhubarb, salad leaves, spinach, squash and pumpkins, sweetcorn, tomatoes

How to choose
Look out for untrimmed vegetables where possible – sprouts on the stalk, peas in the pod, sweetcorn in husks, and so on – as these will keep better. The condition of any remaining leaves is also a good indication of freshness. A few spots are generally fine, but significant discolouration or floppiness is not: broccoli should be a vibrant green rather than yellow, beans and asparagus should snap in half cleanly, and courgettes, marrows and peppers should be firm to the touch.

How to store
Except for squash, which should be kept somewhere reasonably warm and dry, and tomatoes, which do best kept cool but not refrigerated, these vegetables are stored in the salad tray of the fridge and need to be eaten as soon as possible, as the flavour deteriorates rapidly. Keep peas and beans in their pods and sprouts on the stalk until you're ready to eat them, but take the leaves off fennel and rhubarb.

HERBS AND SEASONINGS

basil, bay, chillies, chives, coriander, dill, garlic, ginger, mint, parsley, rosemary, sage, thyme

How to choose
When you're buying herbs, whether cut or potted, look for perky green leaves with no sign of dampness or withering. Stems should be crisp – herbs shouldn't sag if you hold them upright, and they should give off a pleasant fragrance. Fresh ginger root will be sturdy rather than shrivelled, chillies bright and firm, and garlic heads plump and hard with no mould, greenness or sign of sprouting.

How to store
Store cut herbs, chillies and unpeeled ginger in the salad drawer of the fridge, and garlic in a cool, dry, well-ventilated place – it will keep better as a whole head rather than separated into individual cloves. Pots of fresh herbs from the supermarket rarely survive the shock of being moved from the nursery to the shelf, and then your trolley, but give them a fighting chance by repotting as soon as you get home, splitting each plant into several clumps to give it room to grow, and watering only if they seem dry. Position them on a sunny windowsill or greenhouse, and harvest regularly for best results.

STONE FRUIT

apricot, cherry, damson, greengage, nectarine, peach, plum

How to choose
Avoid bruised or otherwise damaged fruit, wrinkles or excessive softness. A deep, rich colour is often, though not always, a useful indication of sweetness: steer clear of any green-tinged fruit in the case of apricots, nectarines and peaches. Ripe fruit will dimple to the touch (a good argument for buying it loose rather than pre-packaged) and may have a tempting scent.

How to store
Keep stone fruit at room temperature to make sure that it's ripe before eating, and if the weather is very warm you may want to refrigerate it once ripened. You can accelerate the ripening process by storing the fruit in a loosely closed paper bag.

HARD FRUIT

apples, pears, quince

How to choose
Think about what you want to use the fruit for – the texture and flavour of apples, in particular, vary hugely, even among the dessert varieties, so it's often worth buying one to try if you're unfamiliar with it. Slight blemishes are fine – indeed, big, perfect, shiny, hard fruit often make disappointing eating, but look carefully for any bruising or insect damage. Ripe quince should be golden in colour, although it will remain hard, so cook before eating.

How to store
Only store fruit that is perfect – an even, lowish temperature with good ventilation makes for the best storage conditions. Make sure you handle fruit with great care to avoid bruising. Ripen at home at room temperature in a dry place – a ripe pear should be slightly tender around the stem but not soft, while an apple and quince will remain firm.

SOFT FRUIT

bilberries, blackberries, blackcurrants, blueberries, figs, gooseberries, grapes, mulberries, raspberries, redcurrants, strawberries, whitecurrants

How to choose
Look for firm, unbruised fruit, and don't be swayed by size or shape: small soft berries often have a more intense flavour than larger cultivated versions. Make a point of sniffing before buying – ripe berries, and strawberries in particular, should be gorgeously aromatic.

How to store
Ripe berries are best eaten as soon as possible, but if you need to buy them in advance, put them in the fridge, then bring them to room temperature a few hours before serving. Wash them very gently if necessary, and dry them thoroughly: berries are delicate and should be treated with respect. Unripe fruit may be left at room temperature to soften.

EXOTIC FRUIT

banana, grapefruit and pomello, guava, kiwi, kumquat, lemon and lime, lychee, mango, melon, oranges and clementines, papaya, passion fruit, pineapple, pomegranate, rambutan, sharon fruit and persimmon, starfruit

How to choose
Select for colour and firmness, rejecting bruised fruit. Exotic fruits are generally sold under-ripe, so you may need to buy them in advance to ripen at home. Both bananas and starfruit turn from green to brown as they ripen, while ripe passion fruit will be purple and dimpled. Citrus fruits, pomegranates and melons should feel heavy for their size, and not look dry or wrinkled; ripe mangoes, sharon fruit and papayas should dimple under pressure, and melons, pineapples and papayas will give off a heady perfume near the stalk end. Choose unwaxed or organic citrus fruit for zesting, and riper yellow-green limes for juicing.

How to store
Exotic fruits should be kept at room temperature until fully ripe – if they ripen faster than you can eat them, put them in the fridge and eat them as soon as possible. Bear in mind that the ethylene given off by ripe bananas will accelerate the ripening process of any fruit or vegetables they come into contact with – a useful phenomenon that you can turn to your advantage.

How to choose and cook beef

British beef has been celebrated for hundreds of years – to understand why, where possible, choose meat from grass-fed, traditional breed animals, which has been hung for at least two weeks. Good beef should be a deep red colour, with a generous marbling of creamy fat.

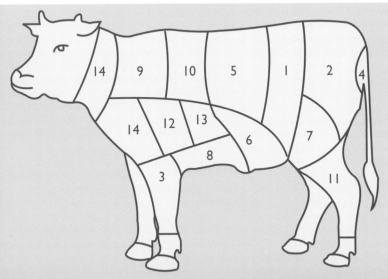

I	RUMP
2	TOPSIDE/SILVERSIDE
3	SHIN
4	OXTAIL
5	SIRLOIN
6	THIN FLANK
7	THICK FLANK
8	BRISKET
9	CHUCK/BLADE
10	FORE RIB
11	LEG
12	THICK RIB
13	THIN RIB
14	CLOD/NECK

CUT	DESCRIPTION	HOW TO COOK
RUMP/ POPESEYE	The rump is the top part of the rear, next to the sirloin – minute steaks and popeseye joints also come from here.	Rump steaks are full of flavour, but can be a bit chewy. Thin-cut minute steaks should be **flash-fried**, and are great for steak sandwiches. The popeseye is a good value **roasting** joint that should be served rare.
TOPSIDE/ SILVERSIDE	Cut from the lower rump and thigh of the animal, the texture of these muscles is testament to the hard work they do moving the cow around.	These are both good **pot-roasting** and **stewing** cuts, although the more tender topside can also make a fine **slow-roasting** joint if it comes from a well-hung animal. Silverside is often used for salt beef.
SHIN/ OXTAIL	Both shin, from the top of the legs of the animal, and oxtail are streaked with connective tissue, and have marrow running through the bone itself. They're also very good value for money.	These cuts demand long, **slow cooking** to break down all that connective tissue, creating a rich, flavoursome gravy around wonderfully tender meat. They are ideal for stews, ragùs and casseroles. On the bone, shin can be used for Italian osso buco.
SIRLOIN	The large muscle from the lower middle of the animal's back, the loin or sirloin produces well known steak and roasting cuts including sirloin, fillet, T-bone, porterhouse, entrecote, wing rib, chateaubriand, fore rib and rib-eye.	All these cuts can stand **fast cooking** at a high temperature, whether **fried**, **grilled** or **roasted**, and are suitable for serving pink.
FLANK/ BRISKET	From the lower chest and belly of the animal, the flank and brisket can be cut into flank steak, short ribs, bavette and skirt steaks.	Most flank cuts are suitable for **stewing**, **braising** and **pot-roasting**, although bavette and goose skirt can also be **marinated** and **flash-fried**. Braised short ribs, long popular in the States, are also becoming increasingly fashionable here. Brisket is the traditional cut for salting.
CHUCK/ BLADE	The shoulder of the animal is a good source of roasting joints and stewing steak. Because it's a well-used muscle, it tends to be tough, and is therefore less expensive, despite its excellent flavour. Available diced, minced or in roasting joints.	Chuck and blade require **long, slow cooking**, whether in a stew or pie, or pot- or **slow-roasted** as a whole joint.
THICK RIB OF BEEF	Confusingly, this cut, from the centre of the animal, is often sold diced as chuck beef or in thin steaks. Thick rib of beef is also referred to as 'leg-of-mutton cut'.	Like chuck steak, this requires **long, slow stewing** or **casseroling** to tenderise it. The steaks should be **cooked quickly** and served rare, to avoid toughness.
CLOD/ NECK	From the chest and neck of the animal, these are good-value cuts often sold as stewing steak, or used in minced beef.	**Long, slow cooking** is needed here – ideal for **braising**, **stewing** or using in pies. Minced stewing steak is suitable for a **slow-cooked** Bolognese-style ragù or chilli con carne.

How to choose and cook lamb

With its distinctive flavour, British lamb, usually from animals under six months old, is among the finest in the world. At its best in late summer and autumn, look for rosy pink meat with white fat.

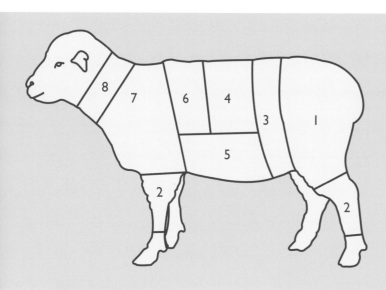

1   LEG
2   SHANK
3   CHUMP
4   LOIN
5   BREAST
6   BEST END/RACK
7   SHOULDER
8   NECK AND SCRAG END

CUT	DESCRIPTION	HOW TO COOK
LEG	The leg is a classic roasting joint, full of flavour and with large areas of solid muscle that yield good steaks, too.	Left on the bone, or boned, rolled and stuffed, leg works well whether **roasted** on a high heat, served pink, or **slow-cooked** until falling apart and tender. Leg steaks and chunks can be **braised**, **stewed**, **barbecued** or **fried**.
SHANK	The knuckle end of the leg – the shank – is a lean, bony cut that needs slow cooking to break down the tough sinew. Sometimes also left on the end of a leg roasting joint.	Done properly, lamb shank can be rich and meltingly tender. This makes it ideal for **braising** or **stewing** in a daube.
CHUMP	The end of the lamb's back, where the loin meets the leg, it's sometimes left on a leg, but makes a neat little roasting joint on its own, sometimes labelled as 'chump end'. Also sold cut into large chops.	Chump is a lean cut, and requires **quick cooking** – either **roasting** at a high temperature, or **fried** or **grilled** over a high heat.
LOIN	The middle of the back, loin is available as a roasting joint, or cut between the ribs into steaks, noisettes or chops. Both loins, attached, make an impressive roasting joint known as a saddle.	A good bone-in roasting cut, loin can also be boned, rolled and stuffed. Delicate little noisettes of lamb, trimmed of fat, are a treat when **fried** and served pink.
BREAST/ FLANK	The breast of lamb, which includes part of the animal's belly, is a fatty cut that nevertheless has a rich, sweet flavour, and is good value.	Because of the fat content, the breast is ideal for **long, slow cooking** such as **pot-roasting**, and is also delicious boned and stuffed. Finish off over a high heat to crisp the fat.
BEST END/ RACK	The first 7 ribs of the back can be divided up into neat little cutlets and noisettes, or left whole as a rack of lamb. Both racks, formed into a circle, make a spectacular crown roast.	Cutlets and noisettes should be **fried** or **grilled**, and racks of lamb **roasted** (see page 184). Both are served pink.
SHOULDER	The front leg of the lamb, this is another classic roasting joint, albeit one less easy to carve. It can also be cut into steaks and cubes.	Because it's tougher, the shoulder should be **cooked longer and slower** than the leg, and served only barely pink. Shoulder steaks and cubes are ideal for **marinating and barbecuing**, or **stewing**.
NECK/ SCRAG END	The neck of a sheep, like any grazing animal, gets a lot of use, which makes this a tough, sinewy cut – but a tasty one, too. Available as boneless pieces or slim bone-in pieces much like oxtail.	**Long, slow cooking** is required here. Irish stew and Lancashire hot pot are two classic neck dishes, but also think curries and tagines.

How to choose and cook pork

This is an incredibly versatile meat – as the old saying goes, 'You can eat all of the pig but his squeal.' Look for outdoor-reared British pork, preferably from a traditional breed, and check that the meat is rosy pink, firm and well marbled with white fat.

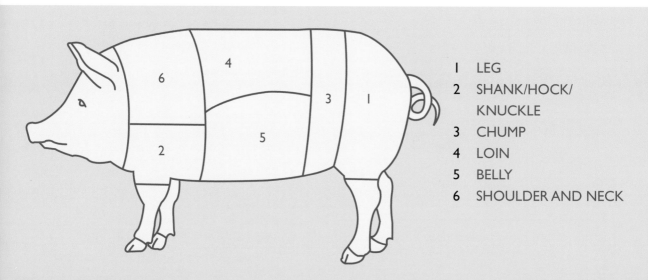

1 LEG
2 SHANK/HOCK/
   KNUCKLE
3 CHUMP
4 LOIN
5 BELLY
6 SHOULDER AND NECK

CUT	DESCRIPTION	HOW TO COOK
LEG	The most popular roasting and curing joint for hams, the leg can also be divided into leg steaks, pork escalopes and diced meat.	Leg is a lean joint, so care must be taken not to let it dry out during cooking. Choose a joint with a good covering of fat and **cook it slowly**, turning up the heat only to crisp the crackling.
SHANK/ HOCK/ KNUCKLE	The lower part of the leg, the hock, is a good-value cut with relatively little meat, but it's big on flavour.	Requires **slow cooking** to render it tender, but as the gelatine melts it gives stews, soups and pot roasts excellent body and flavour. This is also the joint to use for a classic pea and ham soup.
CHUMP	The rear of the back, the chump or rump, is a lean and well muscled joint. It's often sold boned and rolled for roasting (it's moister than the leg) or divided into large, boneless pork chops.	**Roast or pot-roast** a whole joint, or **grill** or **fry** the generously sized chops as you would a loin chop.
LOIN	Runs from the shoulder to the rump of the pig. The first 8 ribs make up an enormous roasting joint known as a rack of pork, but smaller loin joints are more common. It can also be cut into chops or cutlets. The delicate tenderloin (or fillet) should be cooked with care.	Joints should be **roasted**; chops can be **fried** or **grilled**.
BELLY	Generously marbled with fat, the belly is often minced and used in sausages or terrines, but has recently come into its own as a roasting joint. It develops delicious crackling and can be meltingly tender. Streaky bacon is cut from the belly.	Ideal for **roasting**, as the fat keeps this joint moist even as the crackling crisps up. It's also delicious **slow-braised**.
SHOULDER /NECK	A whole pork shoulder is a large, well-marbled roasting joint that's ideal for a crowd. Shoulder and neck can also be diced or minced. Available as boneless pieces or slim bone-in pieces, much like oxtail.	A shoulder joint is best **slow-roasted** and is the ideal cut for making pulled pork. Diced shoulder or neck can be **slow-cooked** or, in the case of the leaner shoulder, **stir-fried** or used for a tagine.

How to choose and cook poultry and game

Chicken, duck, turkey, pheasant and pigeon all come under the banner of 'poultry', as they're kept either for their eggs or for their meat and/or feathers, whereas 'game' is hunted for the pot. It's important to follow good hygiene practices when cooking both. Use separate chopping boards for raw meat and wash hands well after touching raw flesh to avoid cross-contamination. Cook poultry (poussin, chicken, turkey, guinea fowl) until the juices run clear. Game can be cooked until pink, medium or well done, according to preference.

How to joint a chicken

1 Put the bird breast-side down on a sturdy board on a non-slip surface and get out a heavy, sharp knife and kitchen scissors or poultry shears.

2 Locate the 'oysters', or soft patches of flesh on either side of the spine at the top of the legs, and use your fingers to loosen them from the bone.

3 Turn the bird over, and pull one leg away from the body, cut through the skin attaching it and then push down on the leg until the bone comes out of the socket. Cut through the remaining flesh, and remove the leg – the oyster should come away with it. Repeat.

4 Turn the bird over, and place your knife across the holes left by the legs. Cut down between the ribs and the shoulder joint, leaving the wings attached to the breast. Press down on the breasts and pull the back up, so it comes away from the shoulder bones. Separate the two pieces by cutting between these bones.

5 Put the breast skin-side down and slice in two, cutting slightly to one side of the breast bone. Cut the wing sections off at an angle, so you leave about a third of the breast attached to each.

6 To separate the legs, feel for the joint, then make a cut to expose it, and break it with your hands. Cut any sinews still attached. Repeat with the other leg.

7 You should now have 2 breasts, 2 thighs, 2 drumsticks and 2 wing portions.

NB Jointing a duck is similar, but do trim off any large pieces of fat from the carcass. These can be rendered down and used to cook roast potatoes.

HOW TO COOK GAME

VENISON	Seasons vary depending on the species, running from early August to April. Farmed venison is available all year. Venison is very lean: the leg, saddle and loin are great **roasted**, with cooking times depending on the cut. Treat steaks as you would beef, and **pan-fry** until rare, medium or well cooked. Other cuts should be **slow-cooked** in a casserole in a low oven (around 170°C/150°C fan oven/gas mark 3) for around 1½ hours until tender. This meat goes well with redcurrant sauce and juniper berries, but also chilli, chocolate and wine. Extra fat, in the form of streaky bacon, is helpful either way. Allow 150-175g per person.
RABBIT	Wild and farmed varieties are available all year. Lean and gamey-tasting, young rabbit is delicious **roasted**, while older rabbit makes a tasty pie. Wild is superior to farmed, but it's leaner and tougher, so it takes longer to cook until tender. Slowly **braise** for at least 1½ hours in the oven at 170°C/150°C fan oven/gas mark 3 for joints to tenderise. To cook farmed rabbit, follow chicken timings. Joints in a stew should take around 45 minutes, whereas the meat, chopped into small pieces and cooked in a sauce, will take around 20. One rabbit serves 4.
HARE	September to March. **Roast** a young hare or stew older animals – it'll take around 2 hours to ensure that the meat is really tender. Red wine is the classic choice for jugging. One hare will serve 4-6.
GROUSE	12 August-10 December. **Roast** young birds and serve with bread sauce and game chips; older specimens should be **casseroled** or **braised**.
PHEASANT	1 October-1 February. Proceed as for grouse, **roasting** for about 45-60 minutes. Older pheasant makes good curry and stew. One bird will serve 2 people.
WILD DUCK, TEAL AND WIDGEON	Seasons vary depending on species, but run from September to 20 February. **Roast** plump young birds fast at 180°C/160°C fan oven/gas mark 4 for around 40 minutes (mallard), or around 10-13 minutes (teal and widgeon) and serve pink. Scrawny birds should be **pot-roasted** or **braised**. One mallard will serve 2, but allow 1 teal or widgeon per person.
PARTRIDGE	1 September-1 February. **Roast** with a drizzle of oil at 190°C/170°C fan oven/gas mark 5 for 20-25 minutes. Serve 1 partridge per person.
WOODCOCK	1 September (Scotland)/1 October (England and Wales) until 31 January. **Roast** with the innards still inside and the head on at 190°C/170°C fan oven/gas mark 5 for 20-30 minutes, serving 1 per person.
SNIPE	August-January. Treat as for woodcock, serve 1 per person, and **roast** for 15-20 minutes.
QUAIL	Available all year round. Suitable for **quick roasting** (180°C/160°C fan oven/gas mark 4 for 25-35 minutes) or **slow-cooking** in a casserole. Serve 1-2 per person.
GUINEA FOWL	Now farmed, these rich-flavoured birds are available all year round. Treat as for chicken and **roast** at 190°C/170°C fan oven/gas mark 5 for around 1 hour until the juices run clear, or **casserole**. One bird will serve 4.
PIGEON	Both wood pigeon and squab (fledgling pigeons that are reared) are available all year round. It's suitable for **roasting** (brown in a pan first, then cook at 220°C/200°C fan oven/gas mark 7 for 20 minutes) or **braising** for a pie; the breasts are excellent **pan-fried** (2-3 minutes each side) until still pink in the middle. In Moroccan cuisine it's used in the classic pastilla – dense meat combined with a sweet spice filling that is wrapped in filo pastry. Serve 1 roast pigeon per person or 2 breasts each.

All about fish

Fish is a delicious and conveniently easy meal to make at the end of a busy day – it also ticks all the nutritional boxes, too. Look out for bright eyes and firm, shiny skin, and check that there's no whiff other than a faint smell of the sea. Fish fillets should look whole and complete, rather than broken up or mushy. Crab, lobster and mussels should be still alive (unless you're buying frozen) and feel heavy for their size.

ROUND FISH

Anchovies, cod, coley, gurnard, haddock, hake, herring, hoki, John Dory, mackerel, monkfish, mullet (red and grey), pollock, sardines, sea bass, sea bream, sprats, swordfish, tuna, whitebait, whiting

As the name suggests, these are round in cross-section. Larger round fish can be cut into thick steaks across the spine or filleted along either side. Smaller species such as sprat and whitebait are generally cooked and eaten whole.

White fish such as cod, coley, pollock and haddock are very versatile: fresh herbs, white wine and citrus make subtle partners. The firm flesh is ideal for frying, but they can also be baked, steamed, poached or grilled.

Oily species such as mackerel and sardines are robustly flavoured and can take more seasoning: vinegar, smoke and chilli are all good partners. They're also better for grilling or barbecuing, because the oil keeps them moist even over a high heat, but they can also be baked or fried.

FLAT FISH

Fish with the eyes on the top of the body such as brill, dab, Dover and lemon sole, flounder, halibut, plaice, turbot

Smaller flat fish such as sole or plaice are generally cooked whole, but the likes of halibut and turbot are easier to fillet. Whether poached, fried, baked or steamed, flat fish are generally cooked very simply so as not to spoil the delicate flavour. A classic butter sauce, perhaps with capers or fresh herbs, is as elaborate as it should get.

FRESHWATER FISH

Carp, eel, perch, pike, salmon, tilapia, trout

Many fish that come from rivers and lakes have an unfair reputation for tasting 'muddy', yet make good eating. They tend to have firm, meaty flesh that stands up well to stews and sauces, as well as grilling, frying and baking. Try poaching with herbs and other aromatics, or serving them with a zesty green sauce.

SHELLFISH

Clams, cockles, crab, crayfish, Dublin Bay prawns, lobsters, mussels, oysters, prawns, scallops, whelks, winkles

Most shellfish should be bought alive, if possible, to guarantee freshness, and can be stored in wet cloths in the salad tray of the fridge for 24 hours. Oysters can be served raw with a spritz of lemon juice or Tabasco, while clams, mussels and the like will need to be scrubbed well before a brief steaming to open their shells – moules marinière and spaghetti alla vongole are two classic preparations. Crayfish, prawns and scallops can be cleaned, then grilled or fried either in the shell or out of it, while crab and lobster need more careful preparation and cooking, but then can be eaten simply with good mayonnaise and brown bread.

CEPHALOPODS

This category includes cuttlefish, octopus and squid

These may require cleaning, and should either be cooked very fast on a high heat (Chinese salt-and-pepper squid – see recipe on page 90 – calamari and the like) or slow-cooked until tender. Cephalopods can take plenty of of flavour, so be generous with the chilli, herbs or garlic.

The ideal cheeseboard

The principle behind putting together a cheese selection is similar to assembling the ingredients for a great meal: it's all about achieving a balance of flavours from mild through to strong. Here, we've teamed soft and bloomy with washed and aromatic, then thrown in something blue to give a broad sweep of texture and colour. As a guide, allow 100g per person and serve with biscuits, chutney and dried fruit.

Goat's cheese: Golden Cross

Made in Sussex, this young, citrus-fresh goat's cheese has bags of flavour with a faint hint of grassiness. The added texture just underneath the white bloom ('coating') comes from having been rolled in ash.

Hard cow's milk cheese: Caerphilly

When it has matured for around four months, this classic Welsh cheese has a dense, suede-like rind and a hint of translucency on the inside, along with a delicate, meaty flavour and a yoghurt-like freshness.

Hard ewe's milk cheese: Berkswell

This dense, firm-textured Warwickshire cheese has a herbaceous yellow hue, and a delicious sweetness that comes through on the after-bite.

Washed cheese: Golden Cenarth

The vibrant orange shade of this round cheese comes from being washed in a brine solution. It's slightly firm with a fruity sweetness.

Blue cheese: Barkham Blue

Made with Guernsey milk, this blue cheese has huge appeal. There's a pleasing buttery flora to the taste, with a tang of blue coming through it.

Soft cheese: St Eadburgha

This oozy, runny soft cheese with its light, bloomy rind gives way to a mushroomy vegetal flavour. Made in the Cotswolds from cow's milk.

White sauce

For fish pie and lasagne

Put 40g butter in a pan with 40g plain flour. Place over a medium heat to melt the butter. Using a wooden spoon, mix the two ingredients to make a creamy, putty-like mixture. Allow it to bubble for a minute or two, then take the pan off the heat. Gradually stir 500ml warmed milk into the pan and whisk like mad to get rid of any lumps. Put the pan back on the heat, bring it up to the boil and cook for 2-3 minutes more until thickened. Season well.

Ideal Home Show tip:

For extra flavour, first heat the milk in a pan with a bay leaf, a couple of cloves and a few slices of onion. For parsley sauce, stir in 3 tbsp freshly chopped parsley at the end. For cheese sauce, add 100g grated mature cheddar – that's the minimum required to give a cheesy taste, or use half-cheddar and half-Parmesan for a richer flavour.

Hollandaise

For poached fish, or as béarnaise with steak

Put 1 tbsp white wine vinegar in a pan with a bay leaf, a couple of black peppercorns and ½ finely chopped shallot. Bring to the boil and bubble until reduced to a teaspoonful (it won't take long). Pour it into a bowl and add 2 large beaten egg yolks. Place over a pan of simmering water, making sure the base doesn't touch the water. Chop 175g chilled butter into cubes and whisk into the eggy mixture piece by piece. The heat will cook the yolks and start to thicken the sauce. It may become very thick at the beginning, but as you continue to whisk in each piece of butter, the sauce will become smooth. Season with salt.

Ideal Home Show tip:

For béarnaise sauce to serve with steak, stir in 2 tsp each chopped chervil and tarragon.

Mayonnaise

For roast chicken and great burgers

Whisk 2 large yolks in a bowl with 1 tsp cold water. Measure 300ml sunflower oil into a jug. Start to add the oil drop by drop until the mixture begins to emulsify. Once emulsified, you can start to drizzle in the oil, 3 tbsp at a time. Continue to do this until you get a thick mayo. Season with salt and 1 or 2 tsp white wine vinegar.

Ideal Home Show tip:

For tartare sauce, stir in 1½ tbsp each freshly chopped parsley, chives, capers and gherkins and a little squeeze of lemon juice.

Vinaigrette

For green salads, sliced tomatoes and halved avocados

In a bowl, clean jam jar, or dressing bottle, pour 50ml sunflower oil, 50ml olive oil (or extra virgin if you like a punchy taste), 1 tbsp white or red wine vinegar. Scrape in 1 tsp Dijon mustard. Whisk the ingredients together (or put the lid on the jar or bottle and shake furiously). Again, a tiny splash of cold water will help everything come together.

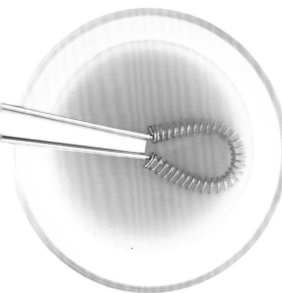

Chilli dipping sauce

For spring rolls and marinated prawns

In a bowl, whisk together 35ml soy sauce, 45ml rice vinegar, 1 sliced garlic clove, ½ finely sliced red chilli (leave the seeds in if you like it hot), ½ finely sliced lemongrass stalk, 1 tbsp toasted sesame oil and a pinch of salt. This is best made at least half an hour before eating so that the ingredients have a chance to marinate.

Salted caramel sauce

For plain cakes, vanilla ice cream and sticky toffee pudding

Dissolve 115g granulated sugar and 75ml water in a pan over a very low heat, taking care not to allow the water to bubble. Bring to the boil and simmer until the bubbling mixture turns a rich golden brown – you'll be able to smell the caramelised sugar. The colour is an important guide to the end flavour. If it's just golden, the finished sauce will be too sweet, but dark brown means it has gone too far and will taste burnt and bitter. Take the pan off the heat and stir in 50ml water. Stand back, as the mixture will splutter like a volcano at this point. If the caramel crystallises, stir the mixture over a low heat to dissolve the bits. Return the pan to the heat and stir in 150ml double cream with a good pinch of salt crystals, and heat through.

Ideal Home Show tip:

For a vanilla caramel sauce, leave out the salt, and scrape in the seeds of a vanilla pod.

Rich custard

For crumbles and poached fruit

Pour 250ml full-fat milk into a pan and bring to the boil. As soon as bubbles appear around the edge, take it off the heat. In a bowl, stir together 2 egg yolks, ½ tbsp cornflour, 40g golden caster sugar and a splash of milk. Pour the just-boiled milk onto the eggs and stir well. Return this mixture to the pan and, stirring constantly with a wooden spoon, gradually bring to the boil over a low heat. As soon as it starts to thicken, stir in 100ml single cream and warm through. But once you add the cream, don't allow it to boil, or it will split.

Ideal Home Show tip:

For a rich chocolate custard, stir in 75g grated chocolate of at least 60% cocoa solids. For a mocha flavour, add 1 tbsp espresso powder at the same time.

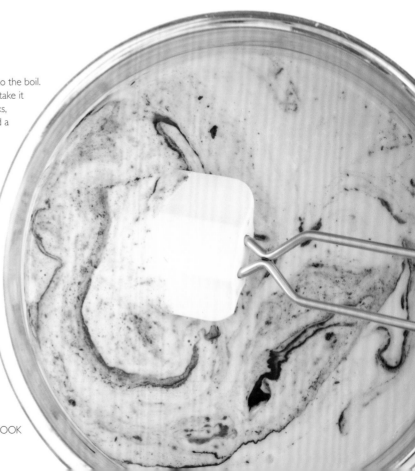

Mango coulis

For ice cream, yoghurt or plain cake

Steady a large mango on a board and cut either side of the stone to release the two halves. Use a knife to crisscross the flesh, then scoop out the cubes, along with any visible flesh, into a food processor. Peel the skin away from the flesh surrounding the stone, then slice the mango off into the food processor, too. Whiz the fruit with a squeeze of lime or orange juice until smooth. If you prefer the coulis smoother, add more fruit juice or a drizzle of water.

Cointreau butter

For spreading on toasted fruit bread, and to go with Christmas pudding

In a bowl, whisk together 100g softened butter and 150g icing sugar, adding the sugar in two batches. Stir in 1 tbsp Cointreau, zest of ½ orange and 1-2 tbsp orange juice. Garnish with extra swirls of orange zest. Chill if not using immediately. It can be stored in the fridge for up to five days.

Farinaceous (pulses, rice and grains)

This is the catch-all term for starchy, carbohydrate-dense foods ('farinaceous' comes from the Latin for flour, '*farina*'), and every item on this list is a food staple somewhere on the planet. They are all relatively inexpensive fuel sources that provide us with energy – but the best thing about them is their fantastic versatility.

Bulgur wheat

This is made by par-boiling dried and ground wheat berries. It has a nutty flavour and is a good source of protein. Rehydrate the grains in hot water or stock. It's the base for Middle Eastern salads like tabbouleh, as well as a handy way of adding bulk to soups and stews.

Noodles

Noodles are long strips of pasta, which can be made from wheat, rice or vegetable flour, and sometimes contain egg. The term is often used specifically for Asian varieties. Cook in plenty of boiling water – timings differ, so always check the packet. Noodles can take the place of rice as a side dish, but are also the backbone of stir-fries such as pad thai and chow mein, or soupy ramens.

Pasta

Pasta is made from a flour (usually durum wheat) and water dough, rolled out and cut into an enormous variety of shapes. Sold fresh or dried, it's sometimes enriched with egg, spinach or other flavourings. It should be cooked in a large pan of boiling, salted water. Fresh pasta cooks more quickly than dried. Many Italian recipes treat pasta very simply, such as the classic carbonara – eggs, pancetta and Parmesan – to more labour intensive sauces like Bolognese, which needs to be slow-cooked to tenderise the mince.

Couscous

Although it looks like a grain, this North African favourite is actually made up of tiny balls of dried wheat dough. Traditionally couscous is steamed, but pre-cooked couscous, which just needs to be soaked in boiling water or stock, is much more readily available now. Served with a knob of butter, squeeze of lemon and a few herbs, it makes an ideal accompaniment to a Moroccan tagine or stew. It also makes excellent salads with roasted vegetables, chargrilled meat and fish.

Polenta

Polenta is ground cornmeal that is sold in fine, medium or coarse textures. Made by stirring it into a pan of boiling water until thickened, it is also served as an alternative to pasta and rice in Italy. You can flavour it with butter and cheese, if you like. Serve immediately, or spoon into a shallow, ovenproof dish, then cut into pieces and fry or grill. Serve topped with roasted or pan-fried vegetables or with rich meat stews. Italians often serve braised game on a mound of soft, creamy polenta.
(see page 170 and 182 for recipe)

Potatoes and tubers

A starchy family of vegetables that includes
yams, cassavas and sweet potatoes. Tubers
cannot be eaten raw, but may be boiled,
baked or fried. A popular side dish, potato
can also take centre stage in dishes such
as tartiflette (the rich and creamy French
potato dish layered with reblochon cheese,
lardons and onions), and tortilla, the Spanish
omelette in which potato provides the
texture against the soft-set egg inside.

Pulses

These are the dried seeds of the legume
family, such as lentils, split peas and beans.
Many dried pulses require pre-soaking before
boiling, whereas lentils can be cooked straight
from dry. Pulses are a good source of protein
and carbohydrate, and are often used to
bulk out soups and stews. They can also be
served as a dish in their own right –
spicy Indian dahl, for example.

Quinoa

A protein-rich whole grain which, before
cooking, looks like little seeds, but turns
translucent once boiled. Quinoa should be
cooked in a pan of simmering water for
about 15 minutes. Occasionally it requires
rinsing or soaking before use. Treat it like rice,
and flavour with oil, lemon juice and herbs,
or use in soups and stews. It can even be
used to make bread.

Rice, white and brown

This dried grain comes in many different forms,
from stubby short grain to long, elegant basmati.
Unpolished brown rice is more nutritious than the
white variety. Boil or steam in water or stock. Rice
can be served as a side dish, but it comes into its
own in biryanis, pilaffs, rice puddings and paellas.

Pearl barley

This important cereal grain is part of the grass
family. Available as pearl, pot or whole hulled, with
the latter the least refined. Treat as spelt (see
below): simmer in boiling water until tender, then
drain and stir a dressing and some herbs through
it to add flavour. Very useful for providing bulk in
soups and stews, and for making into barley water.

Spelt

An ancient variety of wheat, nutty-tasting spelt has
recently enjoyed a revival as a health food. Spelt should
be simmered in water for about 25 minutes until
tender. Use instead of rice in risottos and pilaffs, or try
it cold in salads, and as a thickener in stews and soups.

How to cook an egg

If you can barely boil an egg, then you're about to turn a culinary corner, because this nifty guide will give you all you need to know on the subject. It's handy info, because if ever there was a nutritious and satisfying standby for days when you can't be bothered to cook anything more demanding, it's got to be eggs, the ultimate survival food. Tasty and versatile, they not only go well with a host of other ingredients, they're chock-a-block with vitamins A, D and E, and they're also packed with protein.

boiled

Bring a small pan of water to the boil. There should be enough to cover the eggs by a couple of centimetres, and the pan must be small enough to prevent the eggs from rolling around on the base as they boil. Cook for 6 minutes at a gentle simmer for a white that's set and yolk that's soft and runny. For a hard-boiled egg, cook for 10-12 minutes, depending how firm you like the yolk.

poached

Bring a small pan of water to the boil. Break the egg into a cup (it's best to poach no more than one or two eggs in one go, otherwise the water will be full of white stringy bits). Swirl the water in one direction with a spoon, then gently lower the egg into it. If you're doing two eggs, lower the second one into a separate area of the pan at this point. Poach for about 3 minutes. Lift out with a slotted spoon and drain on kitchen paper.

scrambled

Melt a knob of butter in a saucepan. Beat the eggs in a bowl and season. As soon as the butter has melted, stir in the beaten eggs. Cook over a low-to-medium heat, stirring all the time until creamy. Spoon over a toasted muffin or with ribbons of smoked salmon scattered on top.

omelette

To make one omelette, melt a knob of butter and 1 tsp oil in a 20cm omelette pan. Beat 2-3 eggs in a bowl, season well and, once the butter has stopped foaming, pour into the pan. Swirl to cover the base. Place over a medium heat. The mixture at the bottom of the pan will quickly start to set, so, with a wooden spoon, scrape lines over the base, tipping the pan to allow the runny eggs to pour into them, so that it looks rippled. Cook for a minute or two more until the eggs look just set – they should still be a bit soft. Flip over one edge, then tip the pan and slide the other edge onto a plate. Flip it over again so the fold is underneath. Eat immediately.

fried

Pour about 1 tsp olive oil into a frying pan and place over a low-to-medium heat. Crack an egg into a bowl and slide into a frying pan. Cook until the white is just set. Cover with a lid at this point for 1-2 minutes longer – this will help to cook the egg yolk. Slide onto a plate and serve on hot buttered toast or, for a traditional English breakfast, with rashers of crispy bacon, black pudding and sautéed mushrooms.

Pancakes

prep 5 mins, plus standing time
cook 10 mins

MAKES 6-8

ingredients

125g plain flour
Salt
1 medium egg
275ml milk
Knob of butter
A little vegetable oil
Lemon wedges, to squeeze
over, and golden caster
sugar, to serve

Eggs and butter were among the foods forbidden during Lent, so pancakes used to be eaten on Shrove Tuesday as a way of using them up before the start.

Ideal Home Show tip:
Serve with caramel sauce (see page 290) for an indulgent pudding. For a savoury twist, fill with ricotta and chopped spinach, sprinkle with grated cheese and bake in the oven until warm.

1

Sift the flour and salt into a bowl. Make a well in the centre and add the egg.

2

Stir with a wooden spoon, then pour in the milk, drawing in the flour to make a smooth batter (ignore the odd lump). Set aside for 15 minutes.

3

Heat a tiny knob of butter and a drizzle of oil in a frying pan. Tip the pan to allow the fat to cover the base. Wipe away any excess with kitchen towel.

4

Stir the batter again and pour in a ladleful, tipping the pan around – it should form a thin film that covers the base.

5

Cook for 1-2 minutes until the batter is nearly set on top and the underside is golden. Flip and cook the other side for 1-2 minutes. Transfer the pancake onto a plate and keep warm until you've finished cooking the rest.

6

Continue to cook the remaining mixture until you make 6-8 pancakes. Serve with a good squeeze of lemon juice and a sprinkling of caster sugar.

Individual classic cheese soufflés

prep 15 mins
cook 15 mins

SERVES 4

ingredients

60g unsalted butter
45g plain flour
Pinch cayenne pepper
½ tsp powdered mustard
200ml warm milk
50g mature Cheddar,
 grated
25g Parmesan
4 eggs, separated, plus 1
 egg white

With their soft, fluffy texture and intense hit of cheese, these hot soufflés are as light as air. Made mainly from store-cupboard ingredients, you can knock them up in half an hour, and all they need is a simple green salad to turn them into a light meal. Even better, you can prepare them ahead of time (see tip).

Preheat the oven to 200°C/180°C fan oven/gas mark 6. Preheat a baking sheet. Grease four 250ml ramekins. Melt the remaining butter in a pan, stir in the flour, cayenne and mustard and cook for 2 minutes without browning. Gradually stir in the milk, bring to the boil, still stirring, and cook gently for 2 minutes, beating well to remove any lumps.

Remove from the heat, stir in the Cheddar and half the Parmesan then cool slightly. Gradually beat in the egg yolks. Whisk the egg whites in a clean, grease-free bowl until the mixture stands in stiff peaks. Fold a large spoonful of the whisked whites into the sauce to soften, then, using a metal spoon, carefully fold the rest into the cheese sauce.

Pour the mixture evenly between each ramekin, making sure it comes to the very top. Use a palette knife to flatten the surface. To help the soufflés rise, run your finger or thumb around the edges. Sprinkle with the rest of the Parmesan cheese and stand the dishes on the hot baking sheet.

Bake in the well-heated oven for 12-15 minutes until well risen and golden brown (see right). They're ready when you shake the ramekin and they wobble ever so slightly. Now it's a race against time to serve them before they collapse. Quickly place the risen soufflés on small plates and serve at once.

Ideal Home Show tip:
To prepare ahead, make up the sauce to the stage where the cheese and yolks are incorporated, then cover tightly with cling film. Prepare the dishes. When ready to cook, complete the recipe.

Classic cheese shortcrust pastry

prep 15 mins, plus chilling
cook 15 mins

MAKES 1 PASTRY
CASE

ingredients

175g plain flour
Pinch of salt
110g firm but not hard
  butter
50g extra mature Cheddar,
  finely grated
1 egg yolk

This is a great base for a quiche filling – it also sets the scene for a terrific vegetarian dish: fill with a mixture of ricotta cheese beaten together with chopped herbs, and top with roasted tomatoes.

Ideal Home Show tip:
Steps 1 and 2 can be done in a food processor. Whiz the flour and butter first, and once the egg mixture has been added, pulse the mixture to make a rough dough. For plain pastry, leave out the cheese, and for herb pastry, add 1 tbsp freshly chopped thyme, chives or parsley.

Sift the flour and pinch of salt into a bowl. Add the butter and rub into the flour until it's like fine breadcrumbs. Stir in the cheese. Put the yolk in a bowl, stir in 1 tbsp ice-cold water, then add to the flour mixture.

Stir the beaten egg into the flour mixture with a knife, and bring together with your hands, gently working it into a dough. Shape into a disc, then wrap in grease-proof paper and chill for 15 minutes.

Roll out the pastry, using the paper as a base, until it's a couple of millimetres thick, and line a loose-bottomed, 21cm-deep, fluted tart tin. Prick the base all over, then cover and chill for about 15 minutes.

Preheat oven to 200°C/180°C fan oven/ gas mark 6. Cover pastry with greaseproof paper and baking beans. Bake blind for 10-15 minutes. Remove paper and beans and bake for a few more minutes until dry.

Sweet pastry

prep 15 mins, plus chilling
cook 15 mins

MAKES 1 PASTRY
CASE

ingredients

150-175g plain flour
Pinch of salt
50g golden caster sugar
75g unsalted butter, at
    room temperature
2 egg yolks

A board, some scales and
your hands are all that's
required for this melt-in-
the-mouth sweet, crisp
pastry. Chefs call it pâte
sucrée, because it's made
with a paste of sugar,
butter and flour.

Ideal Home Show tip:
Fruit and frangipane topping turn it
into a to-sigh-for dessert. Or fill with
mascarpone sweetened with maple syrup
and vanilla, and scatter with summer fruit.

Sift the flour and a good pinch of salt
onto a work surface and make a big well
in the centre. Put the sugar, butter and
egg yolks in the middle.

Using one hand, start to 'peck' at the
butter mixture with your fingers, working
all the ingredients together as you go
until they're thoroughly combined.

Draw the flour onto the mixture and
start to work this in to make a dough.
Knead lightly until smooth. Wrap in
greaseproof paper and chill for 30
minutes.

Roll out the dough. Line a 20.5cm shallow
tart tin. Prick all over; chill for 15 minutes.
Cover with greaseproof paper and baking
beans. Bake at 190°C/170°C fan oven/gas
mark 5 for 15-20 minutes until golden.

Chutney

prep 20 minutes
cook 2 hours approx.

MAKES ABOUT 3KG

ingredients

1kg cooking apples
1kg tomatoes
500g plums
500g onions, chopped
200g sultanas
1 tbsp mustard seeds
700ml red or white wine
    vinegar
500g demerara sugar
1 tsp salt

Coming from the Hindi word 'chatni', we have Britain's colonial history to thank for this popular condiment. Late summer/ early autumn is the time for it, when there's a glut of windfall fruit. Simmering the mixture to a soft pulp, then adding the preserving ingredients is the only way to get the texture right. Let it mature for at least a month to allow the flavours to soften and meld.

Prepare the apples: peel, core and chop. Halve the tomatoes, removing and discarding the tough core, and then chop. Halve, stone and roughly chop the plums, and put in the pan with the onions, sultanas and mustard seeds.

Place over a gentle heat and simmer for about 30 minutes until the mixture has cooked down to a pulp. Give the mixture a good stir every now and then.

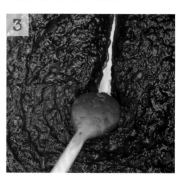

Add the vinegar, sugar and salt, and turn up the heat slightly to bring to a good simmer, then reduce the heat to its lowest setting and let it cook. It's ready when a wooden spoon is drawn through the middle and no excess liquid remains.

Sterilise the jars. Wash well in soapy water and rinse, then dry out in an oven preheated to 170°C/150°C fan oven/gas mark 3. Alternatively, run them through the dishwasher and fill them while still hot. Pot the chutney and cover immediately with airtight, vinegar-proof tops.

Ideal Home Show tips:

- Use this recipe as a base for any other type of chutney you fancy. Combinations that work well are pear and date; peach and dried apricot with a touch of chilli; and marrow, apple and tomato.

- If you want to spice it up a little, think about the softer flavours of the Middle East – coriander seeds, cinnamon, and mixed spice will do the job beautifully.

Simple white bread

prep 30 mins
cook 25-35 mins

MAKES 1 LOAF,
PLUS 8 ROLLS

ingredients

7g dried yeast
Pinch of golden caster
sugar
450ml warm water
675g strong white flour,
plus extra to dust
2 tsp salt
25g butter

Nothing makes us salivate
more than the smell
of a loaf straight out of
the oven. The whole
process is also a terrific
de-stressing mechanism –
and with all that kneading,
it's a pretty good upper-
body workout, too.

Ideal Home Show tips:
- For a light breakfast bread use half-plain, half-wholemeal flour and throw in 2 tbsp seeds (sunflower, pumpkin and linseed all work well).
- For a nutty tea bread use granary flour, then add 175g dried fruit (chopped if necessary) to the recipe above with 2 tbsp golden syrup, and use half-milk in the liquid.
- Toppings: brush with milk or egg for a rich golden crust. Sprinkle with poppy seeds, sesame seeds, bran, or whole-wheat grains.

Sprinkle the yeast and sugar onto the jug of warm water. Set aside for 5 minutes to allow the yeast to activate. Whisk together.

Sieve the flour and salt into a warm bowl. Rub the butter into the flour until it's very fine.

Make a well in the centre and pour in the yeast mixture. Use a round-bladed knife to work the mixture into a 'craggy' dough. Turn out onto a lightly floured surface.

Knead until the dough becomes smooth and soft. To do this, use the heel of your hand or knuckles to stretch and push the dough away, then fold over and repeat.

Halve, and shape one piece into an oval. Cut remaining dough into 8 pieces and shape into rolls or twists. Transfer to a baking sheet lined with parchment. Dust with flour. Leave in a warm place until doubled in size. It's ready when you push your finger into the dough and it springs back.

Bake in a preheated oven at 220°C/200°C fan oven/gas mark 7 for 15-20 minutes for the rolls and 25-35 minutes for the loaf until well risen and golden. To test, tap the bases – they should sound hollow. Cool until just warm.

Chippy-style battered fish

prep 15 mins
cook 15 mins approx.

SERVES 4

ingredients

For the batter
150g plain flour
½ tsp salt
¾ tsp baking powder
225ml beer

To cook
2 litres sunflower oil
Salt and black pepper
4 x 150g pieces white fish

Crisp on the outside with meltingly soft fish on the inside, the great British battered fish supper never fails to raise a cheer. It's important to get the oil really hot, and then to stand well back, as it can spit furiously. Make sure you have a long-handled, metal, slotted spoon to scoop out the fish once it's cooked.

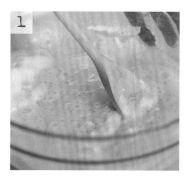

Sift the flour, salt and baking powder into a mixing bowl. Whisk in the beer to make a smooth batter. Set aside for 10-15 minutes.

Pour the oil into a large saucepan and place over a medium heat. Allow to heat up gradually. To test if it's at the right temperature, drop in a piece of bread – it's ready to use when the bread turns golden in 15-20 seconds.

Season the fish, then dip into the batter and coat all over. Using a pair of tongs, drop into the hot oil, one piece of fish at a time, and cook until golden.

Carefully lift out with a slotted spoon and drain on kitchen paper. Keep warm while you cook the remaining fish. Sprinkle with salt and enjoy with chips and mushy peas.

Ideal Home Show tip:
For a very light, Japanese-style tempura batter, replace the beer with iced sparkling water. Add the flour all at once and whisk quickly, taking care not to overwhisk – in fact, it's actually better to leave it slightly lumpy. Use it to coat small pieces of vegetables – cauliflower and broccoli florets, along with carrot batons, work well.

Easy chocolate sponge

prep 30 mins
cook 25 mins

SERVES 10-12

ingredients

For the cake
220g softened butter, plus
    extra to grease
180g self-raising flour,
    sifted, plus extra to dust
180g soft light brown sugar
2 tbsp golden syrup
4 eggs, beaten together
60g cocoa powder, sifted
4-5 tbsp milk
Icing sugar, to dust

For the buttercream filling
50g softened butter
150g icing sugar, sifted
25g cocoa powder, sifted
Raspberry jam

The classic sponge cake is an essential part of any cook's armoury, because not only is it quick to make for afternoon tea, it also conveniently lends itself to being tarted up for a special occasion. Fill with buttercream and jam, dust with icing sugar, and serve. It'll keep in an airtight container in a cool place for up to three days.

Preheat the oven to 190°C/170°C fan oven/gas mark 5. Grease, flour, then line the base of two 20cm sponge sandwich tins with greaseproof paper.

Cream butter and sugar in a bowl until pale. Gradually add the syrup and eggs, alternating with the flour and cocoa until smooth (don't overbeat). Add enough milk to give a soft dropping consistency.

Divide evenly between the two tins, smooth the tops to flatten, and bake for 20 minutes until just firm to the touch. Allow to cool in the tins for 10-15 minutes, then transfer to a rack until cold.

Make the filling. Beat the butter and 50g icing sugar in a bowl. Beat in remaining icing sugar and cocoa with 1-2 tsp water until creamy. Spread jam and buttercream over one cake, then place the other on top. Dust with icing sugar.

Gluten-free lemon drizzle cake

prep 20 mins
cook 50 mins

SERVES 6

ingredients

150g softened butter, plus
  extra to grease
150g golden caster sugar
3 large eggs
100g ground almonds
50g fine polenta
2 tsp gluten-free baking
  powder
Zest of 1 lemon
Juice of ½ lemon

For the topping
Zest and juice of ½ lemon
85g icing sugar

Polenta gives a rich golden colour and a distinctive nutty texture to the sponge, which is then drizzled with sugary lemon syrup. The result is deliciously different, and it's a useful recipe to have up your sleeve for anyone with any kind of gluten intolerance.

Preheat the oven to 180°C/160°C fan oven/gas mark 4. Grease a 20cm loose-bottomed tin and line the base and sides with baking parchment.

Put all the cake ingredients in a large bowl. Beat together until smooth.

Spoon it into the tin, level the top, then bake in the centre of the oven for about 30-35 minutes, or until springy to the touch. Remove from the oven and leave to cool in the tin for 10 minutes.

Make the topping: mix the lemon zest and juice with the icing sugar in a bowl until smooth. Pour over, teasing it over the edges using a palette knife. Leave to soak in, and serve warm or cold.

Strawberry cupcakes

prep 30 mins
cook 15 mins

MAKES 24

ingredients

110g butter, softened
110g caster sugar
2 eggs
A few drops of vanilla
    essence
110g self-raising flour, sifted
2-3 tbsp milk
Strawberry jam

For the buttercream icing
100g softened butter
300g icing sugar
Pink food colouring
12 strawberries, halved

Is there anything more girly than a cupcake? Maybe not, but that doesn't stop the guys wolfing these down. Topped with a fresh, palate-cleansing strawberry, these are dead easy to make.

Ideal Home Show tip:
For chocolate-orange cupcakes, replace 15g flour with sifted cocoa powder. Make the buttercream as directed, leaving out the colouring and adding the zest of ½-1 orange, according to taste. Dust with cocoa to finish, or sprinkle with silver balls or chocolate curls.

Preheat the oven to 190°C/170°C fan oven/gas mark 5. Fill a 24-hole mini cupcake tray with mini paper cake cases.

Cream the butter and sugar together in a large bowl until pale and fluffy. Gradually beat in the eggs and vanilla, little by little, alternating with a spoonful of flour if the mixture looks like it's curdling.

Fold in the remaining flour with sufficient milk to give a soft dropping consistency. Spoon into the paper cake cases.

Put a small spoonful of jam – around half a teaspoon – on top, and roughly swirl with a cocktail stick. Bake for 15 minutes or until just firm to the touch. Allow to cool.

Make the buttercream. Beat together the butter and half the icing sugar in a bowl. Continue to add the remaining icing sugar, then fold in sufficient food colouring to produce a pale pink colour.

Spoon into a piping bag fitted with a star nozzle (we used a C4 nozzle – about 1cm in width). Place a halved strawberry on top, dust with icing sugar and serve.

Simple fruit cake

prep 20 mins
cook 2-2½ hours

SERVES 12

ingredients

175g butter, softened, plus
   extra to grease
150g light brown sugar
3 large eggs, beaten
450g plain flour
Pinch of salt
1 tsp ground mixed spice
450g mixed dried fruit
50g candied peel or glacé
   cherries, chopped
150ml milk
Whole blanched almonds,
   to decorate

So straightforward that
it's child's play – no more
need be said. Enjoy.

Ideal Home Show tip:
You can also listen to your cake: if it's still
cooking, you'll hear a crackling sound!
Store tightly wrapped in clingfilm and foil
for up to five days.

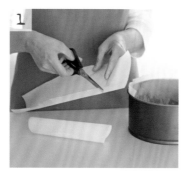

Preheat the oven to 180°C/160°C fan
oven/gas mark 4. Grease and line a
20-23cm springform cake tin with
greaseproof paper.

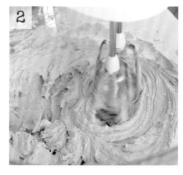

Use an electric hand whisk to beat the
butter and sugar together in a large
mixing bowl until light and fluffy – the
mixture will turn pale once the two
ingredients are incorporated.

Beat in the eggs, a little at a time, beating
well after each addition. If the mixture
looks as though it's going to curdle, beat
in a spoonful of plain flour.

Sieve remaining flour, salt and mixed
spice into the bowl. Tip the dried fruit
and candied peel or glacé cherries on
top, and pour in most of the milk.

Fold everything together, adding more
milk as necessary to give a spoonable
consistency that's not too soft. Turn this
into the prepared tin and flatten the top
with a wet tablespoon.

Cover with almonds and bake for 1½-2
hours. Check that it's not colouring too
much – if so, cover with greaseproof
paper. Cook until firm to the touch, or
a skewer through the centre emerges
clean. Cool in the tin for 10 minutes.

Scones

prep 10 mins
cook 12 mins

SERVES 8

ingredients

225g self-raising flour
Pinch of salt
50g butter
125-150ml milk

Just four store-cupboard ingredients, prepped, baked and ready to eat in less than half an hour, makes a quintessentially British teatime treat. Eat them fresh from the oven, and if there are any left over, wrap them in clingfilm and they'll freeze for up to a month.

Ideal Home Show tips:

- For sweet scones, stir 2 tbsp golden caster sugar into the flour mixture at the end of Step 1.

- For fruit scones, add 50-75g mixed dried fruit, such as currants, sultanas, cranberries and sour cherries, and flavour with orange or lemon zest.

- For cheese scones, stir in 50g mature Cheddar, a good pinch of dry English mustard powder, and a good grinding of salt and pepper.

1 Preheat the oven to 220°C/200°C fan oven/gas mark 7. Sift the flour and salt into a mixing bowl. Rub in the butter until the mixture is fine and crumbly.

2 Make a well in the mixture and pour in almost all of the milk. Bring the mixture together with a knife to make a soft, light dough. If any bits are left in the bowl, use the remaining milk to mix them up.

3 Turn onto a floured surface and knead briefly. Roll out to 2-3cm deep and cut 8 rounds using a 5cm cutter. Re-roll and shape the trimmings, kneading as little as possible.

4 Place on a baking tray and cook in the heated oven until well risen and just firm – about 12 minutes. Leave to cool before cutting and buttering.

Jam

prep 5 mins
cook 30 mins approx.

MAKES ABOUT
1-1.5KG

ingredients

1kg blackberries
1kg granulated sugar
30g butter
25ml vodka, optional

Homemade jam is the real deal – the essence of the fruit shines through and needs only a handful of ingredients. Use granulated sugar for the best clarity, and simmer the fruit in a large pan so that it all cooks evenly. Choose fruit that's high in pectin – blackberries, blueberries, raspberries and gooseberries all perform well.

Put the blackberries into a preserving pan (or a large pan) with 150ml water. Place over a medium heat and bring to a simmer. Cook for 10-15 mins until soft. Chill a couple of saucers in the freezer.

Pour the sugar into the pan and stir over a gentle heat until dissolved. Add 15g butter, put a sugar thermometer in the pan, and bring to a rapid boil. Stir periodically for 10 mins until the jam reaches 103-104°C.

Sterilise the jars. Wash in soapy water, rinse, then dry in an oven preheated to 170°C/150°C fan oven/gas mark 3 for 10 mins. (Or sterilise them by washing in a dishwasher.) Use while still hot.

Test for a set. Take pan off heat. Spoon jam onto saucer. Freeze for 1 min. Run a finger through it – if it wrinkles, it's ready. If not, simmer and test every 5 mins. Stir in 15g butter and vodka. Pot and cover.

Chocolate truffles

prep 10 mins,
plus 2-3 hours chilling

MAKES ABOUT 50

ingredients

250g dark chocolate, at
least 50% cocoa solids
50g unsalted butter
50g sifted icing sugar or
soft light brown sugar
3-4 tbsp brandy, whisky,
liqueur, such as
Cointreau, or orange
juice
150ml whipping cream

For the decoration
Cocoa powder, sifted
Icing sugar, sifted
Approx. 50g almonds,
chopped and toasted

Use the very best quality chocolate for these and go as high with the cocoa solids as you dare. 50% will produce a sweet truffle, while using 70-80% will make them rich and dark with a pleasantly bitter bite. Your popularity rating will soar when you take these round to suppers at friends' houses.

Put the ingredients in a bowl and place over a pan of boiling water, making sure the base doesn't touch the water. Allow the chocolate to melt, and gently stir until smooth and well blended.

Lift it off the pan – use a tea towel to do this, as the steam under the bowl will be very hot. Cool it, then put it in the fridge for 3-4 hours or until set.

Take the truffle mixture out of the fridge. Line a couple of baking sheets with baking parchment. Use a couple of teaspoons to scoop up a little mixture and roughly shape into balls.

Place the balls on parchment-lined trays. If your kitchen is very warm, or your hands are hot, the truffles may melt a bit. So chill them as quickly as possible, then you can reshape them once they're cold.

Put the cocoa, icing sugar and nuts in three separate bowls. Roll each truffle in one or other of the topping suggestions until covered, then put it back on the paper. Chill until ready to serve.

Put a small piece of tissue paper into a box and arrange the truffles inside, reshaping and re-rolling in cocoa, icing sugar or nuts, if necessary.

Tuile biscuits

prep 10 mins
cook 8-10 mins per batch

MAKES 10-12

ingredients

A little sunflower oil
2 egg whites
70g golden caster sugar
Zest of ½ orange
55g plain flour
55g cornflour
Pinch of salt
75g warm melted butter
1-2 tbsp flaked almonds

'Tuiles' is French for 'tiles' – the perfect description for these wonderfully thin, crisp biscuits. Flavour them with any ingredients you have to hand – we've used orange and almond, but ground cardamom and pistachio, coconut and lime, and even rosewater and pine nuts, work well, too.

1

Preheat the oven to 180°C/160°C fan oven/gas mark 4. Lightly grease a rolling pin, and line three baking sheets with non-stick baking parchment.

2

Whisk the egg whites, sugar and orange zest in a bowl until frothy. Sift in the flours and salt, then drizzle butter over and fold in with a large metal spoon.

3

Place teaspoonfuls on the tray at least 10cm apart. With a wet palette knife, spread out to 8cm circles. Sprinkle with the almonds. Bake for 8-10 minutes until the edges are golden. Remove from the oven and cool for a few seconds.

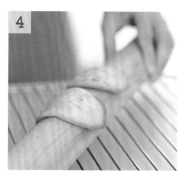

4

Use a palette knife to carefully lift each biscuit off the tray onto the prepared rolling pin. Press onto the rolling pin to shape into a curl. Once shaped, transfer to a wire rack to cool completely.

Ideal Home Show tip:
You can have fun playing with any shape you like. To make a tuile curl, for example, pipe the mixture in a long thin line, and spread with a palette knife until thin, then bake as above. Slide the palette knife under the cooked biscuit, and wrap it around a wooden spoon handle. Let it cool before removing the stick.

The finishing touches

We feast with our eyes before lifting a morsel to our mouths, so it's worth taking the trouble to plate up exquisitely before a special dinner. The key is having all the ingredients lined up ready to use. In general, less is more – don't overload the plate, and frame the food by keeping it well inside the edges. Chill dessert plates to prevent ice cream from sliding around; equally, warm plates before serving hot food. And if you're using garnishes, they should complement the food they are decorating, and be just as edible. Now have a go at these easy tricks of the trade.

Drizzling a sauce

Make a purée with courgettes. Trim the green edges off a courgette (reserve the white flesh for a soup) and chop. Heat a drizzle of olive oil in a pan with 1 smashed garlic clove. Cook for 1-2 minutes just until you can smell the garlic. Whip it out and discard it. Add the courgette to the pan and cook for 3-4 minutes until just wilted. Purée with 50ml vegetable stock and 50ml cream until smooth. Fill a squeezy bottle with the purée. Rest the nozzle on a plate at a 45-degree angle and, gently squeezing the bottle, extract a blob of purée, then quickly drag it across the plate to create the 'tail'.

Smearing a purée

A whoosh of smooth, creamy butternut squash or celeriac purée gives drama to a plate and makes a colourful base for pan-fried fish, meat and vegetable tarts. Cook 200g chopped butternut squash in a covered pan with 50g butter until just soft. Add 100ml stock, bring to the boil and simmer for a few minutes until the squash is very soft. Whiz to a purée. Spoon onto the plate, then draw the back of a spoon through the middle.

Plating up long pasta

Spaghetti, linguine and tagliatelle look impressive when carefully arranged in a bowl. To plate up, drain the pasta, leaving a little water clinging to the strands. Return to the pan and season with a little olive oil or butter. Armed with a carving fork in one hand and large metal spoon in the other, pick up a large spoonful of the pasta. Turn the carving fork round and round so the pasta wraps around it, then carefully lower it onto the plate. Dress with the sauce and serve.

Adding flavour with puréed herbs

Puréed herbs create impact and add a boost of flavour to a finished dish. Blanch 50g parsley in boiling water, then put in a blender with 50g fresh parsley, 50ml olive oil and a pinch of salt. Blitz to make a purée then add a squeeze of lemon to taste at the end. Use a paintbrush to brush over the middle of the plate in a long thick strip. Place vegetable tarts, pan-fried fish or meat on top and serve. Chill any leftover sauce and use within two days. Swirl into soup, or drizzle over buffalo mozzarella or over roasted vegetables.

Making Parmesan crisps

Line a baking sheet with baking parchment. Preheat the oven to 180°C/160°C fan oven/gas mark 4. Grate a chunk of Parmesan. Place a pastry cutter onto the parchment and fill generously with the cheese, making sure all the parchment inside is covered. Lift up the ring and repeat to make as many rounds as you need. Bake in the oven for 12 minutes. Cool on the tray for a minute then lift off carefully with a palette knife and use to garnish soups or salads.

Making vegetable crisps

Crisp and very moreish, deep-fried root vegetables give a flourish of colour and texture on top of a beef stew, or served on soup, and provide a satisfying crunch served with a glass of champagne. Use a vegetable peeler to carve wafer-thin slices from beetroot, potatoes, parsnips and Jerusalem artichokes, then deep-fry in hot oil until golden. Lift out of the oil, drain on kitchen paper and sprinkle generously with salt.

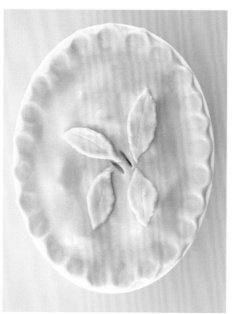

Crimping pastry for a perfect pie

Marking the edge of a pie produces a pleasing finish and helps to secure the pastry to the dish, too. Roll the pastry out on a lightly floured board, place on top of the dish and loosely cut to fit. Using the index finger of one hand, press into the top of the pastry, letting the thumb and finger of the other hand help to create the round shape. For a fluted edge, pinch the pastry between the thumb and finger to make a point.

Stacking roasted vegetables

Sliced aubergines and courgettes griddled until tender with olive oil and layered up with peeled peppers and tomatoes makes for a very easy starter. Cook the vegetables, then cut and shape each piece to fit into a metal ring mould, resting on a board. Slide a fish slice underneath the mould and transfer to a plate. Use the puréed herbs (see tip page 323) as a base. Garnish with basil and serve.

Decorate with chocolate shapes

Melt 50g dark chocolate in a bowl resting over a pan of simmering water, making sure the base doesn't touch the water. Once melted, take the bowl off the heat and cool for 10 minutes. Spoon into a plastic piping bag (or a regular one fitted with a No. 2 writer nozzle). Lay a piece of parchment on a work surface. Snip 1-2mm off the end of the plastic bag and draw lines from left to right to make a rough circle. Turn the paper round and draw the chocolate across the lines to make a crisscross pattern. Repeat to make several more squiggles until all the chocolate is gone.

Make a chocolate collar

Measure the circumference of the cake using a piece of string, add on a 5cm overlap, then measure and cut this length of strip from baking parchment. Make sure the depth of the strip stands a couple of centimetres above the top of the cake. Melt 100g dark chocolate in a bowl resting over a pan of simmering water, making sure the base doesn't touch the water. Once melted, take the bowl off the heat and cool for 10 minutes. Brush the chocolate generously all over the strip and set aside in a cool place until it has dried. Once the chocolate has almost set, lift up the strip and place it around the outside of the cake. Leave to harden. Peel the parchment away from the chocolate.

Making a spun sugar coil

Put 300g granulated sugar in a heavy-based pan with 600ml cold water. Cook gently until the sugar completely dissolves. Put a sugar thermometer in the pan and bring to the boil. Let the mixture bubble until it reaches 155-160°C. Take the pan off the heat; plunge the base into a bowl of cold water. Cool for 3-5 minutes. Oil a knife steel or a wooden spoon handle. Draw a fork through the mixture to pull a strand of spun sugar from the pan. Working quickly, wrap it round the steel or handle, then break off and repeat.

finishing touches

Kitchen equipment

This list isn't exhaustive – it's a round-up of basics with a couple of extra pieces thrown in to help with a few of the more challenging recipes.

Baking beans
Baking sheets
Balloon whisk
Blender or food processor
Boards: several (keep separate boards for preparing
    raw meat, fish and vegetables)
Bowls: small, medium and large
Bun tin
Cake tins: loose-bottomed sandwich tins and springform tin
Can opener
Colander
Cooling rack
Corkscrew
Draining spoon
Electric hand whisk
Fish slice
Fluted quiche tin: loose-bottomed, deep and shallow
Frying pan
Garlic crusher
Grater
Knives and meat fork: chopping, boning or carving knife,
    small paring knife, bread knife
Large metal spoon
Mandolin slicer
Measuring jug
Measuring spoons
Metal skewers
Muffin tin and mini muffin tin
Oven-to-table casserole pan
Palette knife
Piping bags and nozzles
Potato masher or potato ricer
Preserving thermometer
Ramekins
Roasting tin: various sizes, including large for joints of meat
Rolling pin
Round cutters
Saucepans with lids: small, medium and large
Sealable containers: small, medium and large
Sieve
Spatula: small and medium
Tongs
Weighing scales
Wok
Wooden spoons

Oven temperature conversion chart

CONVENTIONAL OVEN	°C	°C FAN OVEN	GAS MARK
Very slow	140	120	1
Slow	150	130	2
Warm	170	150	3
Moderate	180	160	4
Moderate Hot	190	170	5
Fairly Hot	200	180	6
Hot	220	200	7
Very Hot	230	210	8
Extremely Hot	250	230	9

Conversion tables

DIMENSIONS	
Imperial	Metric
⅛ inch	3 mm
¼ inch	5 mm
½ inch	1 cm
¾ inch	2 cm
1 inch	2.5 cm
1¼ inch	3 cm
1½ inch	4 cm
1¾ inch	4.5 cm
2 inch	5 cm
2½ inch	6 cm
3 inch	7.5 cm
3½ inch	9 cm
4 inch	10 cm
5 inch	13 cm
5¼ inch	13.5 cm
6 inch	15 cm
6½ inch	16 cm
7 inch	18 cm
7½ inch	19 cm
8 inch	20 cm
9 inch	23 cm
9½ inch	24 cm
10 inch	25.5 cm
11 inch	28 cm
12 inch	30 cm

WEIGHTS	
Imperial	Metric
½ oz	10 g
¾ oz	20 g
1 oz	25 g
1½ oz	40 g
2 oz	50 g
2½ oz	60 g
3 oz	75 g
4 oz	110 g
4½ oz	125 g
5 oz	150 g
6 oz	175 g
7 oz	200 g
8 oz	225 g
9 oz	250 g
10 oz	275 g
12 oz	350 g
1 lb	450 g
1 lb 8 oz	700 g
2 lb	900 g
3 lb	1.35 kg

VOLUME	
Imperial	Metric
2 fl oz	55 ml
3 fl oz	75 ml
5 fl oz (¼ pint)	150 ml
10 fl oz (½ pint)	275 ml
1 pint	570 ml
1 ¼ pint	725 ml
1 ¾ pint	1 litre
2 pint	1.2 litre
2½ pint	1.5 litre
4 pint	2.25 litres

Spoon measurements are level unless specified otherwise – they convert easily to millilitres and vice versa. But remember, it's only measuring spoons that correspond accurately with these quantities – domestic cutlery may not.
- 1 tbsp (tablespoon): 15ml
- 1 tsp (teaspoon): 5ml

Index

Love the book?
You'll love our events!

Every year tens of thousands of people flock to an Ideal Home Show, looking for inspiration for their homes. These multi-award winning events offer something for everyone, ranging from fabulous kitchens and bathrooms to inspiring room sets and garden designs, sumptuous food, fabulous fashion and even fully constructed houses. All of this content is mixed together with a host of celebrities, experts, theatre shows, cookery demos and so much more. If you're a regular visitor, then we look forward to seeing you again soon. Why not tell your friends to pop along too? And if you've not visited an Ideal Home Show before...where have you been?!

IDEAL HOME SHOW

The Ideal Home Show is held in London and has been every year since 1908, making it the longest running consumer exhibition in the world. Whether you have a substantial home project or want to add those finishing touches that make a house a home, this iconic British Home Show has everything you need! With eight dedicated show sections catering to every requirement and taste, this is the only place to visit when making your home ideal.

www.idealhomeshow.co.uk

IDEAL HOME SHOW SCOTLAND

The Ideal Home Show Scotland, launched in 2011, is an annual exhibition where visitors can shop from over 400 exhibitors offering products not found on the high street in eight different areas of the home. From furnishings and sofas in Ideal Interiors, fabulous food and drink, DIY and kitchens in Home Improvements to planting and outdoor living in Ideal Gardens, there are ideas and inspiration for every aspect of the home.

www.idealhomeshowscotland.co.uk

IDEAL HOME SHOW AT CHRISTMAS

The Ideal Home Show at Christmas brings you everything you need to get your home ready for the festive season. This annual shopping event held in London, brings you ideas on decking the halls, filling your stockings, trimming the turkey, and so much more. This is the biggest home show at Christmas with 600 exhibitors across six sections and is one not to be missed!

www.idealhomeshowchristmas.co.uk

IT'S NOT JUST EVENTS

IDEAL HOME SHOW

We have recently extended the Ideal Home Show brand to help create your 'Ideal life'. This includes the Ideal Weight weight-loss programme, the Ideal Home Show Online Shop, as well as Ideal Home Show Plus insurance, mortgages and the Ideal Home Show Credit Card.

www.idealhomeshowplus.com

Acknowledgements

It was the Ideal Home Show, now owned by Media 10, which provided the inspiration for this book. For over a century now, it has been wowing the public with its ideas and innovations and leading the way in food and cooking trends. Indeed, in latter years, the show's Celebrity Chef Theatre has served to reinforce the show's reputation for creativity by teaching us how and what to cook.

So, Media 10 would like to take this opportunity to thank the many chefs and celebrities who participated in the show: Gregg Wallace, Matt Dawson, Gino D'Acampo, Ed Baines, Jean-Christophe Novelli, Aldo Zilli, Phil Vickery, Dean Edwards, John Burton Race, Theo Randall, Raymond Blanc, Martin Blunos, The Baker Brothers, Richard Phillips, Lily Simpson, Juliet Sears, Olly Smith, Susy Atkins and Mark Lloyd.

Our special thanks go to Nigel Wright, who took what we think is an 'ideal' combination of quirky ideas, easy-to-read recipes and information, and brought them to life with his superb page design. Emma Marsden was unflappable while preparing and cooking every single one of the recipes in this book, ably assisted by Ellie Jarvis. Hilary Ivory, our editor, became expert at understanding our obscure requests. Photographers David Munns and Ruth Jenkinson, with additional photography by Nigel Wright, lavished their creative vision on the pages to brilliant effect. We bow to the skills of chef Stephen Gadd, who gave us a masterclass in how to plate up like a professional, and to Ruaridh Buchanan, manager of cheesemongers Paxton & Whitfield, who provided valuable expertise. We are also grateful to Jerry Green, who made it possible for us to take terrific pictures at New Spitalfields Market. Last but not least, *The Ideal Home Show Seasonal Cookbook* would never have happened without Kerry Garwood's impressive coordination and management skills.

Of course, it goes without saying that no cookbook produced by Media 10 would be complete without Auntie Barb's Sausage Pie (page 236), whose legendary recipe has acquired something of a cult following over the years!